THE HAND OF ADDICTION

The Hand of Addiction maps out addiction from an innovative and holistic perspective, challenging the pervasive discourses surrounding addiction in many fields. Using the metaphor of a hand, the author examines addiction through five conceptual lenses—biomedical, psychological, sociocultural, developmental, and spiritual.

The book successfully integrates Gregory Bateson's understanding of the human hand and further extends it to the study of addiction, studying the relationships between the different fingers (lenses) to reveal how the study of addiction so far has been myopic and compartmentalized. Using an autoethnographic approach, the author constructs a transcontextual mapping of the potential of addiction and challenges what we claim to know about addiction, aiming to understand addiction from a novel perspective. The book also discusses practical strategies that can be used to support those with addiction in various forms.

An important contribution to the literature on addiction studies, this book will be of great interest to academics and postgraduate students in the fields of psychology, sociology, cultural studies, and other related disciplines. It will also be relevant for those interested in the philosophy and ethnography of addiction or those working in mental health.

Weston Robins is President and Founder of Eternal Strength Center for Radical Youth Work. He obtained his PhD in Psychology from the University of West Georgia in 2022. He is currently working in the fields of youth work studies, addiction studies, and broad-based critical psychologies as a researcher, teacher, and clinical practitioner.

Concepts for Critical Psychology: Disciplinary Boundaries Re-thought

Series editor: Ian Parker

Developments inside psychology that question the history of the discipline and the way it functions in society have led many psychologists to look outside the discipline for new ideas. This series draws on cutting edge critiques from just outside psychology in order to complement and question critical arguments emerging inside. The authors provide new perspectives on subjectivity from disciplinary debates and cultural phenomena adjacent to traditional studies of the individual.

The books in the series are useful for advanced level undergraduate and postgraduate students, researchers and lecturers in psychology and other related disciplines such as cultural studies, geography, literary theory, philosophy, psychotherapy, social work and sociology.

Most recently published titles:

Developing Minds
Psychology, neoliberalism and power
Elise Klein

Marxism and Psychoanalysis
In or against Psychology?
David Pavón-Cuéllar

For more information about this series, please visit: www.routledge.com/Concepts-for-Critical-Psychology/book-series/CONCEPTSCRIT

THE HAND OF ADDICTION

A Transcontextual and Autoethnographic Becoming

Weston Robins

Routledge
Taylor & Francis Group
LONDON AND NEW YORK

Designed cover image: Getty Images via Andriy Onufriyenko

First published 2025
by Routledge
4 Park Square, Milton Park, Abingdon, Oxon OX14 4RN

and by Routledge
605 Third Avenue, New York, NY 10158

Routledge is an imprint of the Taylor & Francis Group, an informa business

British Library Cataloguing-in-Publication Data
A catalogue record for this book is available from the British Library

ISBN: 978-1-032-73810-9 (hbk)
ISBN: 978-1-032-73808-6 (pbk)
ISBN: 978-1-003-46632-1 (ebk)

DOI: 10.4324/9781003466321

Typeset in Galliard
by Apex CoVantage, LLC

To my wife Alison, the love of my life and all of eternity. Your support has lifted me to spaces I never imagined possible and you are the most selfless and beautiful soul I have ever encountered, thank you for everything baby. To my daughters, Story and River, you are my heartbeat and bloodflow and not a day goes by that I don't thank God for the gift of being ya'lls father. To my Mom, Jinger Robins, thank you for the trailblazing and showing me that if you work hard enough, you can change the world for the better with your own two hands. To my Grandmother Harriett Magee, your curious exploration and study of psychology paved the way. To my Dad, Jim Robins, thank you for showing me what it means to have an unbreakable work ethic, Stones Rule. To my sister Hana, thank you for always being amazing and loving me unconditionally, best brother and sister team in the world forever.

CONTENTS

FIGURES

TABLES

SERIES PREFACE

Addiction grips you by the throat, throttles you while promising freedom, and is, in this way, rather like the abusive partner who promises to keep you safe while entrapping you all the more. Addiction, among other things, we need to note and keep in mind when we trail through the extensive psychological literature on the topic, is composed of a string of metaphors. A coercive control metaphor is just one of the many we could wield to make sense of addiction, and, if we unravel it, we come to see that it is no more nor less plausible than the other metaphors that undergird the research corpus that Weston Robins takes to task to do something quite different.

This book releases the hand of addiction from our throats and examines that hand, turns the hand itself into a very different kind of metaphor that enables us to think again, look again, at what all this "addiction" that plagues us does (and you will notice another metaphor of viral sickness there in this sentence). Dominant metaphors of addiction are strung together in what some critical psychologists would call a "discourse." What is crucial to remember as we travel through a discourse is that it gives us an illusion of depth, an illusion that there is something that is being described beneath the surface.

The close study of discourse, of the social construction of psychological categories, the stories we are told in the classroom or in a self-help group and that we then tell ourselves, and what critical psychology tells us, is that we need to focus on the surface. And to do that we need critical conceptual resources. This is where Gilles Deleuze and Félix Guattari show their hand, and the metaphor of the hand becomes a device for unraveling and rereading what "addiction" is. Now we are in the realm of a quite new discursive universe of concepts, concepts for critical psychology, concepts that include "assemblage," "planes of immanence," "rhizomes," and "lines of flight." The task is to set out a new cartography of addiction to enable us to map it in such a way as to find a way out.

New concepts for critical psychology, and here the range of terms that the Deleuze and Guattari tool kit offers us, call upon new metaphors to help us read and make sense of the theory as well as the topic. This innovative guide to rethinking addiction works its way inside the discourse of addiction to dismantle it and gives us a space for an experience-near up-close study of how we can develop alternatives to addiction. Meet the band; it includes Deleuze and Guattari and, crucially, center stage, Nora Bateson. She is crucial to the story because she provides a bridge between this array of critical concepts and clinical practice. Family therapy practice is the arena here for us to play out the concepts to make a difference.

So this book is about theory, new developments in family therapy, and the Deleuzo-Guattarian conceptual assemblage, and it is about change, the kind of real change that clinicians working with addiction have been searching for. We are thereby inside the system, rereading claims about "addiction" and taking the metaphors that hold it in place very seriously, and outside that system, playfully opening up new ways of working with addiction through the five fingers of *The Hand of Addiction* that name each substantive chapter. To be simultaneously inside and outside is to be "outwith" psychology, which is where we need to be to make a difference in the lives of people who are in the grip of addiction.

Ian Parker
University of Manchester

ACKNOWLEDGMENTS

First and foremost, I am deeply indebted to each of the members of my dissertation committee: my chair, Kathy, and my thoughtful readers Hans and Tobin. In particular, I want to thank Hans and Kathy for all you have done in my life. Your support academically has been unwavering, but even more importantly you have changed the way I see the world and how I move through the world. Hans and Kathy, your deep wells of knowledge, creativity, and insight have been woven into my soul and reverberate in all I do therapeutically, academically, and professionally, thank you! Lastly, I would like to acknowledge my mentors and guides who have paved the way and given me unwavering support and guidance. Phil Foster, LPC, you have taught me more than you will ever know, and I carry you in my heart. David MacLeod, LPC, thank you for helping me embark on the journey of becoming a therapist. Dr. Joanne Peeler, thank you for carving sacred space and always showing me the way. Dr. Jody Iodice, thank you for believing in me and seeing my potential. Dr. Damond Logsdon, thank you for your continual support and for teaching me so much. Thank you Dr. Pete Williams, for allowing me space to take the deep dive into unconscious exploration and toward holistic growth. And lastly, thank you Dave Herz, you were right the kids do love the tattoos!

1

INTRODUCTION

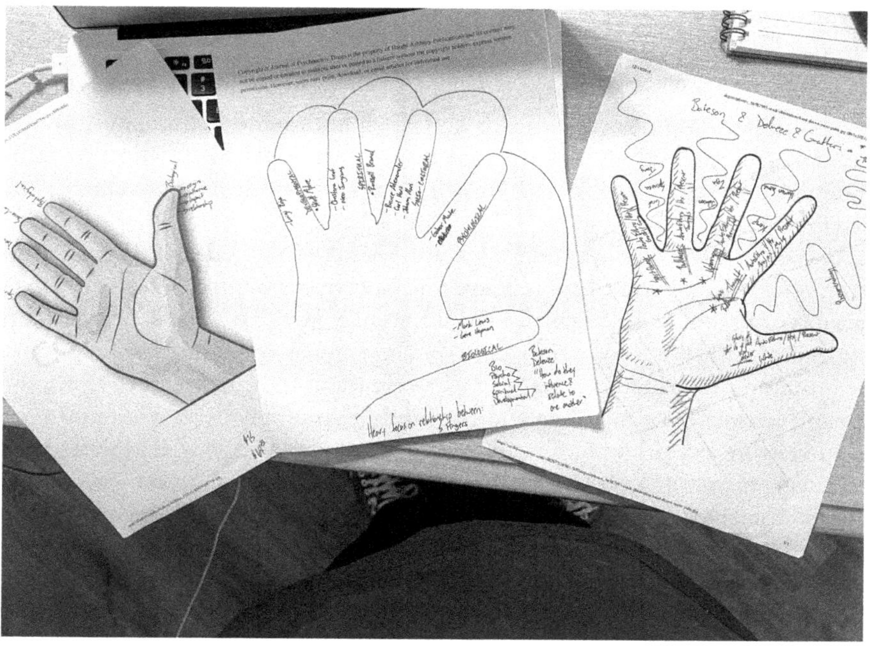

DOI: 10.4324/9781003466321-1

When I was 15 years old, my dad took me to see jazz pianist Herbie Hancock perform at the Variety Playhouse in Atlanta, GA. I was nowhere near prepared for how much this experience would impact me. I can still remember picking a seat up front and waiting patiently for the show to begin. Herbie came out and sat at a grand piano as two other musicians took the stage with him, one playing a stand-up double bass and the other, percussion and drums. The next two hours were pure bliss. I closed my eyes and let the sounds and vibrations wash over my soul. It was a language speaking to me, a dance moving me, a movement pulsating throughout me. The explosion of soul, groove, funk, and improvised jazz swam throughout my soul, and for a moment I was one with everything; there was no separation between me, the music, the vibrations, the musicians, their hands, the instruments, the air, the particles . . . all were woven together in a unitive bliss. Pure spontaneity and child-like play as the piano sang and danced among the bass showering over the driving tempo and pulsation of the drums. In my lifetime, I have seen over 150 live music performances, and nothing has even come close to that night, ever.

My Project

In this project, I aimed to move the examination, study, and discourse of addiction to a new level of exploration, understanding, and thought. My goal was to impact and inform all fields and disciplines of addiction study and to influence all institutions and organizations working with addiction to think differently about addiction and what it does and can do, its movement, and assemblages.

There are many avenues and trajectories for how to approach this goal; however, my project is one of soundscape and improvisation: to seek, to create, to get lost, and find myself again and again, to play jazz! To write as if I am playing music and to let my words flow off the page as resonating sonic booms, penetrating the reader's senses, and allowing them to hear, see, feel, taste, and touch the essence of my truth and to reveal the multiplicity of addiction.

In viewing my project as an improvisational jazz trio, I utilize three players/instruments: (a) on the *drums*: Gregory and Nora Bateson; (b) on the *double bass*: Deleuze and Guattari, who are my backbone, my rhythm section, and the core foundation of my epistemological and ontological framing; and (c) on the *piano*: me, an autoethnography—the arena of my lived experience with addiction and the phenomenological thread woven into the rhythm foundation. All three work and improvise together, their voices in engagement and relationship with the other. My project is a jazz piece, alive, exuberant, and unfolded as a process of improvisation. As Sal Paradise described the jazz band in Jack Kerouac's (1957) *On the Road*:

> [T]hey writhed and twisted and blew. Every now and then a clear harmonic cry gave new suggestions of a tune that would someday be the only tune in

> the world and would raise men's souls to joy. They found it, they lost, they wrestled for it, they found it again, they laughed, they moaned and Dean sweated at the table and told them to go, go, go.
>
> *(p. 230)*

This project is my tune, my song, my melody, my heart on a platter, my thoughts, my emotions, and my skin and bones revealed and examined, jumbled and shaken up, picked apart, and put back together to reveal the tales of my days and the story of our lives. The autoethnography, my piano melodies and highlights (the stories and narratives of my lived experience), ecological and relational systems (G. Bateson, 1972; N. Bateson, 2016), and the plane of immanence and *A Thousand Plateaus* (Deleuze & Guattari, 1980/1987) represent my drums/percussion and the double bass rhythm section. My hope is that this unique and exploratory recording of my soul—one filled with speeds, rhythms, tonality, tempo, melody, and harmony—becomes not just a document but rather an experiential piece others can utilize for their own music. I invite theorists, musicians, academics, artists, and all brave explorers to play along with and amplify the theoretical framework and sound of *The Hand of Addiction: The Spaces In-Between, An Autoethnographic and Transcontextual Becoming*.

Ecological Systems Thought

As an anthropologist, philosopher, psychologist, ecologist, and cyberneticist, Gregory Bateson was an explorer of life and nature. He felt that these titles and academic fields were no different from one another and believed that nature and life itself would never separate these fields. Therefore, he was a profound thinker who contributed to and influenced a wide range of fields of study through his work. His works—*Steps to An Ecology of Mind*, *Mind and Nature: A Necessary Unity*, and *Angels Fear: An Epistemology Towards the Sacred*—reveal a unique epistemological and ontological framework. He focused on systems and their continual relationships with and influence upon each other. He knew that nothing could be separate from anything else and therefore studied the patterns, connections, and the spaces in between phenomena, recognizing these areas to be of immense importance to the integral nature of being.

Nora Bateson, Gregory's daughter, is a filmmaker, writer/educator, and a brave warrior explorer who upholds her father's intellectual legacy through an ongoing engagement with his work. Her work brings the fields of biology, cognition, art, anthropology, psychology, and information technology together into a study of the patterns in the ecology of living systems. In particular, *Small Arcs of Larger Circles: Framing Through Other Patterns* is a woven tapestry of personal reflection, academic examination, and sociocultural commentary focused on a revolutionary approach to systems study and complexity. Gregory and Nora Bateson's work and thought were integral components in my project and mapping of addiction.

In the current field of addiction studies, most researchers and theorists study addiction through one conceptual lens, each with their own specific epistemological and ontological assumptions (Oksanen, 2013). Between and among these lenses of study, there is limited crossover or examination of how each lens influences the others, and there is a great deal of controversy in the field regarding which one best represents the cause and experience of addiction (Miller & Carroll, 2006; Orford, 2002; Robins, 1993; West, 2006). Consequently, there is a lack of theoretical ideas that enable researchers to combine findings from the social sciences, psychology, and neurology (Oksanen, 2013). In this project, I raised questions about the relationship/s between these lenses.

In *Steps to An Ecology of Mind*, Gregory Bateson discussed the importance of such relationships using a metaphor of the human hand. While it is easy to see how the human hand has evolved through our embryology into a structure with five separate fingers, the hand was once a webbed unit, he explains, and the four spaces between the fingers were just as important as the fingers themselves. He encourages us to explore conceptual lenses and how they operate, but also—and in even more depth—how these lenses operate *in relation to one another*. If we were to conceptualize addiction studies as a human hand, assigning conceptual lenses of addiction to each of the five digits or fingers, then that model might look like this: the thumb (biological), the index finger (psychological), the middle finger (sociocultural), the ring finger (developmental), and the pinky (spiritual). Currently, addiction researchers view each finger separately.

In 2016, Nora Bateson wrote of a similar segmentation of knowledge, using the term "mental mono-cropping" to describe how researchers and theorists in singular fields generate ideas that are designed to be resistant to cross-pollination. It is only when we recognize the grand interconnectedness of all systems, she argues, that we can begin to better understand ourselves and the world we continually co-create. This "[m]ental mono-cropping is imprisonment," she tells us, "Emancipate the ideas and they will burst into co-evolutionary bloom in a nearly unreadable knot of spiraling influences" (N. Bateson, 2016, p. 19). Both Gregory and Nora Bateson push us to think about relationships between systems at play rather than simply studying singular, specialized lenses.

In this project, I look to their work to "emancipate the ideas" and study the spaces between the fingers of addiction to propose that until fields of addiction research and study work transcontextually, addiction specialists will continue to see and examine addiction through myopic lenses and fail to recognize its holistic manner. My goal is to push researchers away from the study of addiction as a stagnate entity and to embrace addiction as a living, moving, and breathing energy which can be studied vis-à-vis a relational understanding that explores the spatiotemporal and biopsychosocial–spiritual lenses relationships to and influence upon one another. Gregory and Nora Bateson serve as the first portion of my tool kit of thought (drums and percussion), and Deleuze and Guattari's work and conceptual theories contribute to the remaining portion of the rhythm section (double bass).

The Deleuzo-Guattarian Tool Kit

Gilles Deleuze and Félix Guattari's work, *A Thousand Plateaus*, offers many conceptual tool kits to explore and examine existence and life. Deleuze's *Difference and Repetition*, Guattari's *The Machinic Unconscious*, and their joint work, *Anti-Oedipus, A Thousand Plateaus*, and *What is Philosophy?* pave new ways to think, explore, and understand philosophy, existence, and human behavior. Throughout my project, I employed a Deleuzo-Guattarian vocabulary and conceptual tool kit to break open and map the field of addiction study and examine the organic nature of addiction itself. While I wove this language into my writing to illuminate a new way to think about addiction as a whole, the following is a brief catalog of the main concepts I employ throughout my work: plane of consistency, plane of immanence, arborescent, rhizome, molar/rigid, molecular/supple, segmentarity, strata, stratification, assemblage, multiplicity, line of flight, territorialize, deterritorialize, reterritorialize, etc. Here, I briefly define and expand on three of these concepts.

Plane of Immanence. The plane of consistency and the plane of immanence are vast and largely comprehensive ways to understand "what is." The planes are all-encompassing and nothing can exist outside of them. The plane of immanence constitutes "the absolute ground of philosophy, its earth or deterritorialization, the foundation on which it creates its concepts" (Deleuze & Guattari, 1991/1994, p. 41). The plane of immanence is the image of thought, prephilosophical, neither a concept nor the concept of all concepts; the plane is formless, unlimited absolute, neither surface nor volume, but always fractal (Deleuze & Guattari, 1991/1994, pp. 33–36). Concepts are birthed, created, formed, exist, crumble, and die on the plane of immanence. Concepts are the waves, and the plane is the ocean.

Rhizome. Scott and Marshall (2009) stated that a rhizome is "[a] complex botanical metaphor for a non-hierarchical organizing structure based on a horizontal root that grows through the soil sprouting new plants" (p. 370). As an alternative to tree-based structure, a rhizome features "radical asymmetry, random distribution, and interconnectedness [which] means that it cannot be understood in terms of binary compositions, consequently it resists categorization and structural analysis" (Scott & Marshall, p. 370).

Deleuze and Guattari challenged the linear and arborescent/tree-like conceptualizations of mainstream Western philosophy and metaphysics, designing instead a schizo or rhizomatic/free-form, boundary-piercing model. Scott and Marshall (2009) noted the following:

> Deleuze and Guattari start by opposing the rhizome to the root-tree, arguing that Western metaphysics has always manifested a basic preference for roots and trees over stems, flows, and rhizomes. The tree presupposes the notion of a single pivotal tap-root or foundation out of which all structures are produced by way of binary division (or what they call the process by which the One becomes Two and Two becomes Four and so on).
>
> *(p. 4)*

Deleuze and Guattari were interested in challenging thought and pushing the boundaries of cognition to see concepts in a new light and understand them in relation to one another. By thinking rhizomatically, we can engage with a flux of intensities and free-flowing ideas. The rhizome can help us think more openly and challenge systems of linear rigidity. The rhizome can offer a more radical understanding of ontological processes as dynamic and mutating assemblages (Scott & Marshall, 2009, p. 4).

Finally, the rhizome is a subterranean stem, free from roots and radicals, as is the potato or any organic structure in which each point is necessarily connected to each other point, in which no location may become a beginning or an end, yet the whole is heterogeneous. Deleuze (1968) labeled the rhizome as a "multiplicity" rather than a "multiple," wrestling it from any relation to "the One" (p. 8). Likewise, the rhizome resists structures of domination (Clinton, 2003).

Lines. Deleuze and Guattari discussed three types of lines in their work that impact all of life. The first two lines are lines of segmentarity and lines of subjectivity. Lines of segmentarity (or control) are either supple or rigid. Supple segmentation is molecular, while rigid segmentation is molar. Rigid segmentation is clear-cut and binary, a series of exclusive disjunctions—either this or that—with no in-between. Supple segmentation on the other hand is looser and more flexible and maintains molecular capacities. Supple segmentation allows lines to bifurcate freely and develop in new directions and from all directions without being tied to a centrality. The more molecular or flexible the line is, the more it is open to change (Deleuze & Guattari, 1980/1987).

While the molar/rigid line creates binary distinctions and the supple line creates codes and territories, a third type of line—the line of flight—deterritorializes and decodes. All of society and culture can be mapped according to these lines. Both macro and micro politics can be dissected according to Deleuze and Guattari's lines. In this project, I used the lines to map addiction and demonstrate the ways in which society has shaped the concept with lines of segmentarity and subjectivity.

Deleuze and Guattari offered many creative openings of thought through which addiction can be examined and analyzed in a new and much-needed capacity. Deleuzo-Guattarian philosophies offer and provide academics the opportunity to examine the relationship between various theories and to traverse the gaps in between. Rather than continuing to hunt for and find the etiological root of addiction, for which there is none, Deleuzo-Guattarian theory allows for more in-depth analysis and a mapping of addiction as a continually produced process, which is both situational and interactional (Oksanen, 2013).

Deleuze and Guattari (1980/1987, p. 7) were interested in the notion of process or flux. Examining the potentiality and manifestation of concepts rather than merely defining them, Deleuze and Guattari's *Schizoanalysis* is a complex philosophy in which they advocate for a deterritorialization of thought. To think schizo or rhizomatically means to break barriers and walls of molar and rigid stratification with molecular intensities that offer potential lines of flight. Using a Deleuzian approach, I explore not "what addiction is," but rather "what addiction does and how it moves." Utilizing this theoretical entry point, I examine what addiction can do, along with how it continually shapes and reshapes society, subject, object, and behavior in a perpetual and recursive feedback loop.

Deleuzian Cartography: Make a Map, Not a Tracing

Building on the works of Coonfield and Oksanen, I break the linear and moral/rigid philosophical and psychological studies of addiction and employ the Deleuzo-Guattarian tool of cartographic mapping:

> The map is open and connectable in all of its dimensions; it is detachable, reversible, susceptible to constant modification. It can be torn, reversed, adapted to any kind of mounting, reworked by an individual, group or social formation. It can be drawn on a wall, conceived of as a work of art, constructed as a political action or as a meditation.
>
> *(Deleuze & Guattari, 1980/1987, p. 12)*

To look at how addiction functions and how it has grown and reshaped over time is key. We must not merely try to continue to answer the question of what addiction is. Springboarding from Deleuze and Guattari's concept of constructing a map, I believe in a mapping of addiction, not a tracing—an exploration in contact with the real, a performance, a fostering of connections, a removal of blockages, a maximum opening to an understanding of addiction. Understanding addiction as rhizomatic allows us to enter the concept of addiction at any point and dimension to truly understand it and how it moves. The map of addiction is itself part of the rhizome. Coonfield (2008) stated, "In terms of the social milieu to which it is connected, a map is an *abstract diagram* that makes visible spatio-temporal relations such that acts of location, movement, and flow become possible in new ways" (p. 83).

I examine particular lenses through which researchers study, conceptualize, and understand addiction (i.e., biological, psychological, sociocultural, developmental, and spiritual). However, as maps do, I show the terrain, interplay, gaps, fissures, and crossovers of the landscape. Rather than drawing borders around the lenses of addiction study, I reveal how each lens bleeds over, into, influences, and impacts the others because, organically, there is no separation between and among them. More accurately, these are unique ways language divides and traces various elements of the process and flow we call addiction. Coonfield (2008) stated,

> Cartography—the practice of making maps—is a practice of imagining relations between forces, differentiating formed matters and expressions, organizing the visible and the expressible, which in turn organize and regulate the social field to which the map is connected.
>
> (*p. 83*)

My project examines the relationship between each lens to better understand the holistic entity that is addiction and ultimately to show how these borders and constraints have been socially constructed to further split and detach addiction from its true rhizomatic nature. Coonfield (2008) continued:

> Deleuzian cartography is not about tracing correctly or incorrectly in order "to describe a *de facto* state" (Deleuze & Guattari, 1987, p. 12). To map is to experiment, to create a way of seeing and speaking that is "open and connectable in all of its dimensions; it is detachable, reversible, susceptible to constant modification."
>
> (*p. 12*)

In mapping and exploring the hand of addiction, I further examine the relationship, interaction, and influence of each conceptual lens of addiction theory to create a new way of seeing and speaking about addiction. Treating addiction as a multiplicity that is rhizomatic in nature, I ultimately examined how addiction connects assemblages of linguistic codes, micro-political struggles, power relations, biology, and art. Deleuze and Guattari (1980/1987) stated,

> A multiplicity has neither subject nor object, only determinations, magnitudes, and dimensions that cannot increase in number without the multiplicity changing in nature (the laws of combination therefore increase in number as the multiplicity grows). Multiplicities are defined by the outside: by the abstract line, the line of flight or deterritorialization according to which they change in nature and connect with other multiplicities.
>
> *(p. 8)*

Moving ahead, it will become evident how addiction itself is a multiplicity, neither subject nor object, only flows of intensity changing in nature and being shaped by other flows of intensity. Addiction is constantly in flow, moving, weaving, becoming, ultimately deterritorializing and reterritorializing throughout history. Mapping addiction, I reveal its flux of energy and intensity. In addition, I propose ways out of rigid substance abuse (lines of flight, deterritorialization, becomings, nomadology and war machines, crevices, and openings) to bypass the striated and controlling conceptualization of the state apparatus. Addiction is a molecular multiplicity on the plane of immanence, leaving it open to molar rigidity or smooth, unstriated, and unsegmented space. If we can redirect addiction to other endeavors, addiction can offer a true line of flight from substance abuse.

Self/Autoethnography

As the methodology of autoethnography continues to grow and develop, scholars in various fields of study have taken it up in several different ways. Ethnography (i.e., the study of culture) takes its roots and origin from Anthropology. Autoethnography is the integration of the self (auto) or subjective lived experience in a cultural analysis or examination (ethnography). There are many variations and subfields of autoethnography. However, they are all constructed on some combination of cultural analysis and autobiography. Ellis and Bochner (2000) observed that [a]utoethnographers vary in emphasis on the research process (graphy), on culture (ethno), and on self (auto). Chang (2008) noted that autoethnography should employ an ethnographic methodology, an interpretive orientation where culture is at the forefront and finally its overall content should be rich with autobiography.

Why Autoethnography. In *Handbook of Autoethnography*, Ellis et al. (2013) described five main purposes for autoethnography: (a) disrupting norms of research practice and representation; (b) working from insider knowledge; (c) maneuvering through pain, confusion, anger, and uncertainty and making life better; (d) breaking silence, reclaiming voice and "writing to right"; and (e) making work accessible. With this framework and purpose, I chose to use autoethnography as both a methodology and a way of life as a researcher, psychologist, and human soul.

Although I can imagine researching addiction using other methods, autoethnography itself seems to be the only tool/methodology that allowed me to explore and examine my own past lived experience of addiction while simultaneously examining and analyzing the sociocultural components of addiction along with current theories and research in the field of addiction studies. My ultimate goal was to utilize my subjective and internal experience of addiction to maneuver through and examine addiction as a broader cultural concept that impacts and affects large numbers of individuals in modern-day Western society. Employing an autoethnographic study of my lived experience of addiction is truly the only way I could envision creating a comprehensive and holistic examination of addiction.

By observing and studying the relationships between the fingers/lenses and the spaces in between them, we can begin to not only understand addiction in a new way but also rethink much of what we claim to know about addiction. Chapter 2 is the beginning of the journey through the hand of addiction via the thumb (biological). In each subsequent chapter, I will examine another digit in the hand of addiction, index finger (psychological), middle finger (sociocultural), ring finger (developmental), and pinky (spiritual). In doing so, I broaden our understanding of addiction and ultimately reveal how the organic nature of addiction has been compartmentalized and continually severed throughout various fields of study.

Utilizing the ecological and systems framework of Gregory and Nora Bateson (drums) and Deleuze and Guattari's (double bass) vast tool kit of conceptual thought, as well as my lived experience, autoethnography (piano), to play a new tune and unveil new understandings of addiction. In doing so, I attempt to challenge the field of addiction study to view addiction as a transcontextual becoming, molecular organizational flux, a rhizomatic fusion of sound washing over, and being continually birthed from the plane of immanence. This is *The Hand of Addiction: The Spaces In-Between, an Autoethnographic, and Transcontextual Becoming* (see Figure 1.1).

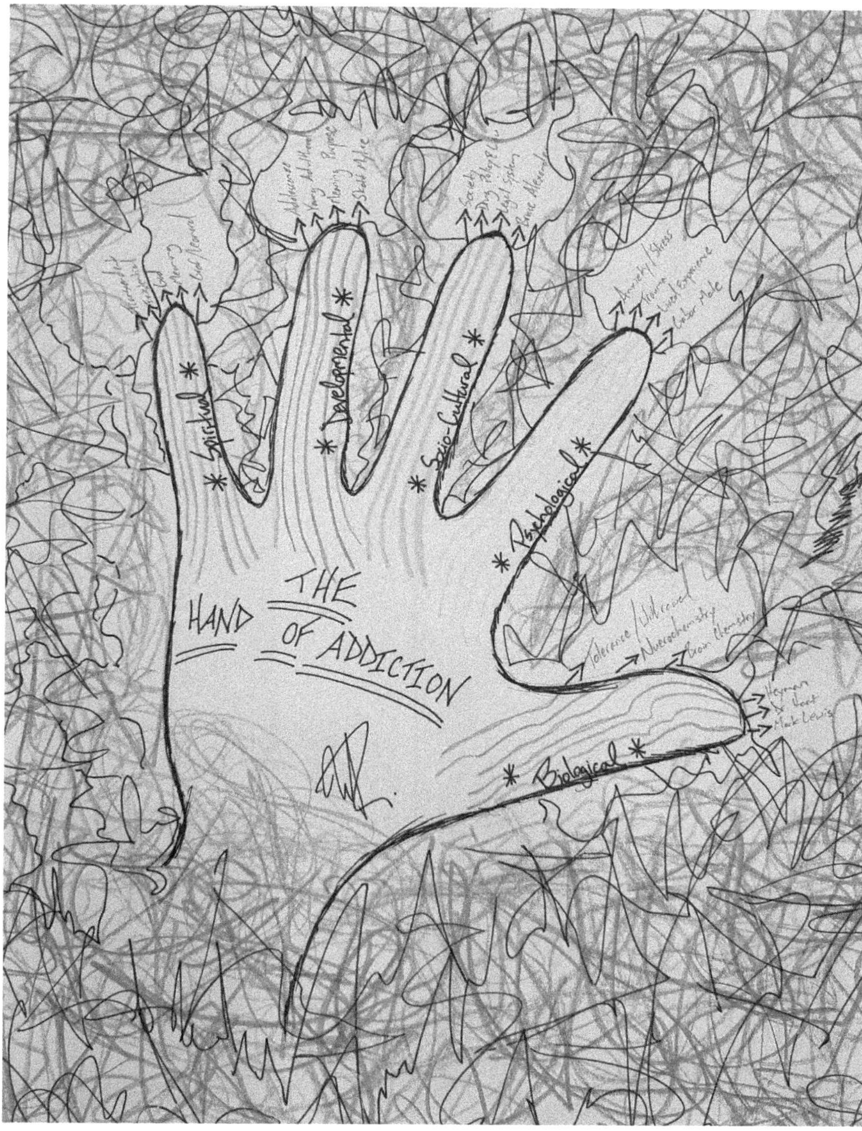

FIGURE 1.1 The Hand of Addiction

2

BIOLOGICAL—THE THUMB

DOI: 10.4324/9781003466321-2

Hi, My Name Is Wes, and I Am Infinite Possibility

I can still remember sitting in my first court-mandated Alcoholics Anonymous (AA) meeting. I had been arrested and given 1-year probation, which included attending 90 AA meetings in 90 days. As the meeting began, each person went around the room and began to share their story. The first sentence everyone spoke was, "Hi, my name is ____, and I am an alcoholic and an addict." I can still recall the immediate visceral and the highly resistant internal response I had to this. I thought to myself, "I may be immersed in addictive patterns and behaviors, but my identity is not defined solely as this behavior." At the same time, however, I recognized that the role and goal of AA was to help individuals move away from denial and move toward acceptance. Although I reluctantly said the phrase, "Hi, my name is Wes, and I am an addict," so that I was not ostracized, I knew in my heart that I was not an addict and that I was a subject full of unlimited potential.

I now recognize that my earlier intuitive response was a fight for freedom, a battle cry stating, "I am not one thing, I am not diseased, I am not biochemically broken." I was more than willing to take responsibility for the fact that I was unhappy, lost, disconnected, and overwhelmed; however, admitting to addiction seemed an insult to the multitude of personality and characteristics comprising my being. I may have been willing to state, "Hi, my name is Wes, and I am a son, brother, artist, spirit, soul, human, and lover; and, I am struggling with addiction and substance abuse." Saying that I was an addict implied a stagnating identity that would never change and had always existed in my being. I would always be a son, a brother, an artist, spirit, soul, human, and lover; however, being an addict seemed like a label that I resisted because I knew that I did not identify this with an intrinsic aspect of self.

My use of heavy stimulants, cocaine, and methamphetamine lasted for approximately two years. I was a daily user of these stimulant substances, and they radically shifted every aspect of my life. I did not consider myself an addict nor did I believe I had a brain disease which would plague me for the remainder of my life. In the biochemical model of addiction (Hammer et al., 2013, p. 28), theorists describe the exact opposite of my lived experience. The biomedical model of addiction claims that my genetic predisposition and my engagement with substance use combined to abnormally structure my biochemistry, and therefore, I am subject to living with the disease of addiction for which there is no cure. I believe the biomedical model of addiction is helpful in that it has allowed for the study and examination of how drug use and genetics make up, inform, influence, and change brain structure. However, it is frequently utilized to oversimplify addiction to a biological etiology.

I would argue that the dialogue of addiction must begin to move away from concrete claims about what addiction is and more toward the examination of what addiction does. Addiction is all-encompassing. It influences and impacts a person's brain, body, psychology, development, and social and spiritual life. The concept of addiction as a disease is concerning in regard to how it shapes an individual's view of self around an illness. For instance, no one says, "I am cancer," "I am diabetes," "I am AIDS," or "I am heart disease." Instead, they say, "I have cancer, I have diabetes." If I walked into a doctor's office and received a diagnosis of cancer, I would have no problem saying, "I have cancer." However, I would take issue with saying, "I am cancer." I have an understanding that cancer is only one facet of my identity. It does not encapsulate my being. I am willing to admit I have an addiction, as I believe many individuals do, but we are never only one thing; we are a multitude of patterns and characteristics which are continually growing, shifting, and moving. As Jungian analyst Robert Johnson (1986) wrote:

> None of us is just one thing. We are not monodimensional creatures; we are rich combinations of the infinitely varied archetypes. Each of us is part heroine or hero and part coward, part parent and part child, part saint and part thief. It is learning to identify these great archetypal motifs within ourselves, learning to honor each one as a legitimate human trait, learning to live out the energy of each in a constructive way, that we make inner work a great odyssey of the spirit.
>
> *(pp. 34–35)*

Beginning to view addiction as a mode of subjectivation rather than a product of biochemical forces can help gather a deeper understanding of how addiction operates. We must recognize and become aware of the complex play of forces that influence and impact many contemporary modes of subjectivation with a focus on addiction in this project. But first, we will examine the origins of the biological field of addiction study.

History

The National Institute on Drug Abuse (NIDA, 2020) defined addiction as "a chronic, relapsing disorder characterized by compulsive drug seeking, continued use despite harmful consequences, and long-lasting changes in the brain" (para. 1). Overall, the notion that addiction is a brain disease has a long and arduous history. As White (2000) explained:

> It took a lot to birth a disease concept of alcoholism in America. A breakdown of community norms that had long contained drunkenness in colonial America and a shift in consumption patterns from fermented beverages to distilled spirits led to a dramatic (nearly three-fold) increase in alcohol

> consumption between 1790 and 1830. In the face of these changes, several prominent individuals "discovered" addiction and called for a new way of understanding and responding to the chronic drunkard.
>
> *(p. 2)*

In outlining this breakdown, White (2000) examined the early works of Anthony Benezet, Benjamin Rush, Lyman Beecher, Samuel Woodward, and William Sweetser and how each played a role in laying the foundation for the disease concept of alcoholism.

The "first articulation of a disease concept of alcoholism by an American physician" (White, 2000, p. 3) can be found in Dr. Benjamin Rush's (1784) work, *An Inquiry into the Effects of Ardent Spirits Upon the Human Body and Mind*. Rush was adamant that abstinence was the only cure for the disease of alcoholism and went so far as to suggest that a nation corrupted by alcohol could never truly be free. Rush challenged the traditional viewpoint at the time—that alcoholism reflected moral depravity or mental illness. Rush believed that alcoholism should be viewed as a self-contained disease, thus marking one of the first times a member of the medical community conceptualized addiction through a lens of pathology.

In his treatment of this disease, Rush drew on the medical science of the day. During Rush's time, physicians operated under the notion that good health was a result of balance among the four humors or bodily fluids (i.e., blood, phlegm, black bile, and yellow bile; White, 2000, p. 4). Rush's (1805/1947, pp. 16–17) treatment approach to excessive alcohol use consisted of numerous attempts to balance the body humors, including inducing perspiration and vomiting, inducing fright, and even bleeding the patient. In many ways, Rush's work on alcohol abuse set the stage for the development of cognitive neuroscience and the biomedical framework for studying addiction.

Although Rush was the first American physician to articulate the concept of excessive alcohol use as a disease, it was Swedish physician, Magnus Huss, whose 1849 study birthed the term alcoholism. Huss noted:

> These symptoms are formed in such a particular way that they form a disease group in themselves and thus merit being designated and described as a definite disease. . . . It is this group of symptoms which I wish to designate by the name Alcoholismus chronicus.
>
> *(White, 2000, p. 5)*

Americans were beginning to form and shape their understanding of addiction as a disease during this time period. Language and discourse regarding addiction had begun to influence every facet of society/culture and how they viewed, treated, conceptualized, and defined substance abuse.

During the 19th century, immigration, industrialization, and expansion into the Western frontier resulted in a xenophobic paradigm of substance use (White, 2000). Accordingly, much of addiction and its rules, regulations, and tolerance directly correlated with societal beliefs about race, culture, and morality. The temperance movement emerged from this set of beliefs as a means of conceptualizing and attempting to treat alcohol abuse and early temperance and recovery movements were almost always white, Protestant, anti-Catholic, and often anti-immigrant (Yates & Malloch, 2010, p. 18). As America grew in culture and population, the concept of alcohol abuse expanded as a reflection of these changes. I will speak in greater detail about the sociocultural aspects of addiction study in Chapter 4.

Though the temperance movement founders initially encouraged individuals to moderate their alcohol use, they quickly determined that abstinence was the only way to regain healthy communities and families within society. White (2000) reflected, "The temperance movement's advocacy of abstinence rather than moderation reflected both a growing understanding of what would later be christened addiction—this recognition of craving and compulsion not controllable by personal will" (p. 7).

In addition, the medical community increasingly began to view addiction as a disease, negative illness, malady, and sickness. T. Trotter, an Edinburgh, UK physician, wrote in his *Essay, Medical Philosophical, and Chemical, on Drunkenness and its Effects on the Human Body* "the habit of drunkenness is a disease of the mind" (White, 2000, p. 8).

In the late 1800s, some communities constructed inebriate homes and asylums in an attempt to treat what would later be referred to as addiction (Baumohl, 1990). In 1867, several texts dealing with approaches to addiction treatment began to appear in the *Journal of Inebriety* under the editorial guidance of New York physician T.D. Crothers. By the late 1800s, these inebriate homes became the site of the first professional movement to medicalize excessive drinking and drug use in America.

As physicians and medical institutions began to reconceptualize addiction as a disease, they challenged the once-popular cultural model of addiction as a product of sin, vice, indulgence, and habit (White, 2000). Addiction, once seen holistically as either a moral failing or the product of weak will, was now seen through a medical lens, offering a radically new and different understanding of habitual substance use. Furthermore, opium use and Chinese immigration began to be named as causal factors for the increase in addiction in the 19th century. As Americans experienced infectious diseases and painful medical disorders, physicians also began utilizing morphine to treat ailments and the pain caused by them. White (2000) stated,

> The oft-times indiscriminate dissemination of opiate-laced medicines by physicians, the pervasive presence of a predatory patent medicine industry,

> and such technical developments as the isolation of morphine from opium and the introduction of a perfected hypodermic syringe all contributed to a rise in narcotic addiction. Whatever suffering medicine could not cure in the 19th century, morphine and the hypodermic syringe could alleviate.
>
> (*p. 8*)

As society reframed addiction in the context of opiates, the concept of the individual having little ability to control their use became more prevalent. However, both biomedical and spiritual theorists continued to battle over whether chronic opium use was an uncontrollable disease or just a destructive habit or vice. White (2000) stated,

> This conceptualization of "morphinism" as "a disease of the body and mind," while still poorly developed and quite controversial, began to move into the mainstream medical literature slowly. Simultaneously, addiction to alcohol and other drugs were embraced within a new term, *inebriety*, that captured a wide variety of drug choices, patterns of use, and types of resulting problems.
>
> (*p. 9*)

Addiction was in its earliest form of conceptualization. Throughout the remainder of the 19th century, society continually understood addiction through three conceptual lenses. The first framework was that substance use was a vice, habit, or sin, and the behavioral choice of use and continuation of use fell ultimately into the hands of the individual (psychology). The second was that the substance or drug itself contained properties, which, once ingested, hooked or addicted the individual (biology/physiology). The third was that societal influences—mainly in the medical arena (physicians and pharmacists) and in the distilleries (saloons/bars)—were the cause of addiction (sociocultural; White, 2000). Although addiction was being viewed through each of these lenses, they were continually seen as separate and in a constant "one or the other" mental conceptualization (White, 2000).

We can still see the impact and influence of these early concepts of addiction today. In these early studies, proponents for the biomedical and spiritual lenses of addiction began to split and create opposing views on how our culture viewed addiction. The cultural legacies of xenophobia, racism, and classism shaped much of the languaging from these proponents. By compartmentalizing and languaging addiction as a physiological allergy, a brain addiction, and a moral failing/sin, our culture entered into a long-term battle to definitively answer the question: What is addiction? It is this original division of addiction concepts that has continued to plague the field even over a century later.

In the early 1900s, psychoanalysts such as Sigmund Freud, William Stekel, Ernst Simmel, Sandor Radó, and Karl Menninger began to view substance abuse as a maladaptive behavior with psychological underpinnings (Yalisove, 1997). The disease concept of addiction began to fall by the wayside (White, 2000)—a reconceptualization exacerbated by the closure of treatment centers and the emergence of laws banning the nonmedical use of drugs and substances. Supreme Court decisions and state and federal laws and regulations replaced physician treatment of addiction with criminal charges and sanctions of the addict (White, 2000, p. 16). Many people began to view "[a]lcoholics and addicts, once 'patients' worthy of sympathy" as "moral weaklings and criminals" or "dangerously insane" (White, 2000, p. 14). In the field of mental health, psychiatric practitioners subjected addicts to abusive and experiential treatments via "often lethal withdrawal regimes, psychosurgery (prefrontal lobotomies), chemical and electroconvulsive therapies and drug therapies that eventually included barbiturates, amphetamines, and LSD" (White, 2000, p. 15).

In 1937, the work of William Silkworth caused a resurgence in the addiction-as-disease model that would foreshadow future and pivotal work in cognitive neuroscience. Silkworth (1937) argued that alcohol abuse is a disease characterized by specific symptomatology and a fixed diagnosis of a specific and chronic pathology. Moreover, he described alcoholism as an allergy of the body and an obsession of the mind while observing a sequence of symptoms patients experienced during a period of four to six months. Those symptoms included alcohol cravings, complete loss of appetite, insomnia, dry skin, hypermotor activity, and anxiety.

Silkworth (1937) went on to make addiction treatment recommendations based on abstinence. Refraining from alcohol use, he suggested, would allow an individual to revitalize and normalize their cells. Moreover, Silkworth encouraged individuals suffering from addiction to allow their intelligence to override their emotions by conceptualizing alcoholism as a physiological allergy. Ultimately, Silkworth played a significant role in influencing and impacting Bill Wilson during his own treatment and recovery. Wilson would go on to found AA.

AA History

On May 18, 1939, in Cleveland, Ohio, AA held its first official meeting (White, 2014, p. 127). Currently, most AA and Narcotics Anonymous groups adhere to a brain disease model of treatment, but Wilson originally viewed alcohol from more than one conceptual lens.

White (2000) quoted Bill Wilson's response in 1960 when he was asked about AA's position on the disease concept:

> We have never called alcoholism a disease because, technically speaking, it is not a disease entity. For example, there is no such thing as heart disease. Instead, there are many separate heart ailments or combinations of them.

> It is something like that with alcoholism. Therefore, we did not wish to get in wrong with the medical profession by pronouncing alcoholism a disease entity. Therefore, we always called it an illness, or a malady—a far safer term for us to use.
>
> *(p. 16)*

Wilson's core understanding of the AA mission has been lost in translation quite a bit in the current AA model. Many current AA leaders use a cognitive neuroscience and biomedical lens to view alcoholism as a brain disease—albeit a brain disease with a spiritual cure. White (2000) explained:

> AA's use of medical terms reflects not an observation on the source or nature of alcoholism but its belief about the solution. When Wilson asked Dr. Bob Smith, AA's co-founder, to comment on the accuracy of referring to alcoholism as disease or one of its synonyms, Smith scribbled in a large hand on a small sheet of his letterhead: "Have to use disease—sick—only way to get across hopelessness."
>
> *(p. 16)*

AA initially used the disease concept, not as a medical fact but, rather, as a tool to enforce and emphasize the deadliness of the condition. Although it was initially used to help the addicted individual recognize they were powerless and needed help and support to break their addiction, it ultimately provided a basis for AA's current understanding of addiction as a brain disease.

The formation and growth of AA further fueled and emphasized the disease model of addiction, which had another resurgence in the mid-20th century. The modern alcoholism movement and work of Dwight Anderson and Marty Mann—along with the Research Council on Problems of Alcohol, the Yale Center of Alcohol Studies, and the National Committee for Education on Alcoholism—all had an enormous influence in reframing the study and treatment of addiction as a sickness rather than a vice (White, 2014, p. 130).

During this earlier period of addiction study, many researchers were concerned that addiction was being seen and understood myopically. Psychologist E.M. Jellinek, for example, explored the growing popularity of the disease concept of addiction, warning of the dangers of viewing addiction through a medical lens alone. White (2000) stated, "Jellinek's concern reflected that of other scientists who, even as the disease concept was being culturally embraced, feared a future day of reckoning for this simplistic portrayal of alcoholism" (p. 19).

The 1980s saw a tremendous surge in treatment programs, hospitals, and privatized drug treatment centers with care models founded on the disease concept of addiction. Additionally, the disease concept of addiction was used as a framework of understanding for many other drugs besides alcohol (White, 2000). This concept also impacted concepts of drug use in fields such as the law, medicine, religion, education, business, labor, and media. As the 20th century ended, proponents and critics of the disease concept of addiction continually battled against one another.

Present Day

Researchers who study brain chemistry, physiology, neuroscience, and biomedical psychiatry have all taken hold of the phenomenon of addiction and named it a complex brain disease for several reasons. One continued argument of those in the biomedical is that because substance and drug use changes the structure of the brain, it can be defined as a *brain disease* (Heyman, 2010, p. 23). However, addiction is still vast and complicated because of the many variables that impact and affect its manifestation. Genetics, biochemistry, and neurology greatly influence the occurrence and perpetuation of addiction; however, this can also be said for any human condition (i.e., anxiety, depression, obesity, and diabetes). Addiction must be examined and distinguished as a complex phenomenon, and we must not allow it to be boxed in primarily as a disease model conceptualization. Any human condition can be traced to biochemical, genetic, and brain chemistry; however, we must recognize this is merely one language through which we can speak about a highly complex phenomenon. Coonfield (2008) observed this about the biomedical model of addiction:

> The disease or medical model . . . assumes that "the etiological agent," a pleasure-producing substance or behavior, "interacts with a susceptible host," one that is genetically predisposed to "initiate the disease process" by imbibing the substance or engaging in the behavior concerned. The effects of substances and behaviors are understood as chemical events in the brain, rather than as a means for medicating a defective ego. And effective treatment requires a chemical intervention, which the authors claim is analogous to "vaccinations for infectious agents," to prevent the chemical events that produce pleasure and craving from occurring.
>
> *(pp. 83, 89)*

As a result of this model, society now sees addicts as helpless and predetermined subjects who, innately and organically, carry the disease of addiction in their biological makeup. Furthermore, addiction is treated as a disease that can be cured or treated only through abstinence from substances. However, abstinence-based treatment is further problematized by the compounding and countless multiplying substances or behaviors (video games, sex, food, gambling, social media) to which one can become "addicted."

Rather than contribute to another discourse and dialogue of the biomedical model of addiction's efficacy, I ultimately wanted to examine the thumb's (biomedical) relationship and engagement with other models/fingers of addiction (psycho/social/developmental/spiritual) study to illuminate how we, as a society, take up and treat both the conceptualization of addiction and our deeper understanding of addiction as a whole.

Magnetic Fields of Force

In his study, "Mapping Addicted Subjection," Coonfield (2008) examined four intensive zones that make up and contribute to the biomedical/biophysical pole of addiction. He utilized a field concept in which he explored magnetic fields of force and intensive zones. Pulling from a scientific model of fields of force, Coonfield built on the work of Ebert, examining the phenomenon of magnetism. Recognizing that negative and positive forces attract while homogenous forces do not, Coonfield (2008) stated, "I want to argue that from the 'field' perspective I am articulating here, what matters is the relation between them" (p. 87).

Coonfield (2008) was interested in studying the relationship between the forces and arenas of addiction rather than merely continuing the age-old tug-of-war between medical and moral conceptualizations of addiction. Coonfield (2008) noted,

> I consider ways in which moral and bio-physical polarizations of addiction discourse attract and repel certain meanings, descriptions, explanations, and practices concerning addiction. It is by way of these that a field of possibilities and responsibilities for addicted subjection is produced.
>
> *(p. 90)*

Although my examination of addiction included many more poles and intensive zones beyond the biomedical zone, I used a cartographic approach to explore the relationships between and among zones (biological, psychological, sociocultural, developmental, and spiritual). What is necessary is the recognition that addiction is "an electric or magnetic field," a zone of intensity, a rhizomatic, schizo, nomadic becoming (Deleuze & Guattari, 1980/1987)—not just in the biomedical zone, but everywhere.

Intensive Zones Within the Bio

Coonfield's (2008) diagram of zones included the pharmacological zone (the forces of substances); the pathological zone (the diseased body); the neurological zone (the brain and nervous system); and the evolutionary zone (forces such as heredity and genetics). Each zone, though different in its focus, still traces and ties the root of all addiction to a biological core.

In the pharmacological zone, Coonfield (2008) described the influence of the substances themselves, stating that once an individual engages with an addictive substance, he or she will crave the substance in a process of continued tolerance and withdrawal. Herein lies the basis for the notion that if an individual engages with opiates, cocaine, or methamphetamine even one time, he or she will become hooked, and addiction will take hold of his or her mind.

In the pathological zone, Coonfield (2008) described the influence of the body itself as the source of addiction—even before an individual has engaged with any substance or drug. Here, Coonfield (2008) drew on Silkworth's work on addiction as an allergy to contextualize addiction in the language of pathology, wherein the body has a natural and negative reaction to substance use that results in addiction. In the neurological zone, Coonfield discussed the individual's nervous system and links addiction directly to a person's tolerance of extraneous stressors and their impact on one's nervous system capacity. He explained:

> It was believed that individuals had finite amounts of nervous energy and that adverse social or environmental stresses (associated with "modern life") depleted one's energy. Once depleted of nervous energy, individuals turned to "stimulants" like opiates and alcohol for temporary rejuvenation. In doing so, the individual became susceptible to the opium or alcohol habit.
>
> *(Coonfield, 2008, p. 95)*

In contemporary neuroscience, researchers continue to focus on and examine the impact of dopamine and pleasure centers of the brain, along with areas of the brain associated with learning, behavioral patterns, and choice theory. However, as Coonfield (2008) noted, these theories may "imply different discourses, different forms of practice, different 'problematics,' and different cultural and historical situations, they nevertheless look to related *neurological* forces as a determinant in explanations of drug habits and addictions" (p. 95).

In the fourth intensive zone, Coonfield describes the evolutionary determinants of addiction. Many researchers have attempted to uncover a single chromosomal explanation for addiction through the identification of a genetic vulnerability, nervous instability, an "alcoholism gene," or overall heritability toward addiction. Additionally, evolutionary theorists have proposed that dopamine is linked to learning, and therefore, we have evolved to pursue pleasurable activities. Coonfield (2008) noted "that dopamine links behaviors to learning, and that these linkages have species consequences: it is what makes 'eating, having sex, and mothering infants'—all activities necessary for the species to continue—pleasurable and worth repeating'" (p. 96). In other words, Coonfield argued that drug use hijacks and takes over the learning and reward pathways in our brains.

In stepping back and looking at the four intensive zones in the biomedical model of addiction, it is still troubling what this work neglects in describing addiction. Although the biomedical model of addiction may help us understand the relationship between drug use and physiology, neurology, pathology, and evolution, biomedical theorists fail to consider the relationship between drug use and an individual's sociocultural environment, psychology, developmental growth, and spirituality.

In addition, we must begin to break open the thought space around addiction and use language and tools that allow us to think altogether differently about it. We see the importance of the language used in describing addiction in shifting and influencing how people understand and feel about addiction overall. Deleuze and Guattari (1980/1987) helped us understand when they reconceptualize arenas and lenses of cognition and biochemical neurology:

> Thought is not arborescent, the brain is not a rooted or ramified matter. What are wrongly called "dendrites" do not assure the connection of neurons in a continuous fabric. The discontinuity between cells, the role of the axons, the functioning of the synapses, the existence of synaptic microfissures, the leap each message makes across the fissures, make the brain a multiplicity immersed in its plan of consistency or neuroglia, a whole uncertain, probabilistic system ("the uncertain nervous system").
>
> *(p. 15)*

By reconceptualizing biochemical cerebral functioning as rhizomatic and schizo in later chapters, we can better understand and conceptualize the organic nature of cognition and neurological impulse functioning. Historically, biomedical theorists in addiction studies have framed addiction as a brain disease or physiological ailment that marks an individual as broken or biologically damaged. Based on this understanding, we may conclude that addicts do not have "normal" brain and synaptic functioning us to believe that addicts.

Addiction as a Mode of Subjection

Coonfield (2008) focused on the importance of moving away from an individual conceptualization of addiction, writing:

> I am interested in addiction as a *mode of subjection*, not a thing or an entity but mobility involving heterogeneous forces and discourses in the ongoing organization of addiction as a modality of a social being. My use of the term addicted subjection (rather than addicted subject) is more concrete, in that it focuses on the ongoing accomplishment of a mode of social being in the relations, meanings, practices, and lines of force that compose it, rather than on the subject as a *fait accompli* . . . as a reified and abstract entity.
>
> *(p. 85)*

The biomedical model of addiction reinforces the concept of an addicted subject and largely views and conceptualizes addiction as an epidemic of the individual. We must be cautious because continuing to focus on the addict as the *subject* fails to recognize the complex and cosmic play of forces that create and perpetuate addiction. Coonfield (2008) wrote:

> Addiction is paradigmatic—perhaps even the apogee—of subjection as Deleuze explains it. For addicted subjection is constituted as a mode of individuation authorized by the power-knowledge of clinical judgment ("You are an addict")—which would include the "self" disciplines of psychology, psychiatry, substance abuse treatment, and medicine—and by the addict-subject's own confession ("I am an addict"), as embodied for example in the "self-help" of group-based recovery therapies.
>
> *(p. 82)*

My project included a continuation of Coonfield's (2008) examination of the spread of addicted subjection, of "the addict" as a particular, pathologized kind of subject. Additionally, my study focused on how biological, psychological, sociocultural, developmental, and spiritual fields continue to produce the mode of subjection we name addiction.

Relationships and Interplay

The biomedical model of addiction is of utmost importance to observe, study, and explore how our neurology, brain chemistry, and physiology influence and are impacted by addiction. It is not the influence of neurochemistry, brain physiology, and brain chemistry that I negate. Rather, it is the rigidity and closed borders of these fields and disciplines (or the mental monocropping; N. Bateson, 2016) that concern me and that I deconstruct in the following chapters. The biomedical model of addiction fails to recognize and consider the relationship and influence of other conceptual lenses of addiction (psychological, sociocultural, developmental, and spiritual; Hammer et al., 2013).

While a thumb is an integral component of the hand, it does not comprise the hand. Similarly, while the biomedical model of addiction is a core component of addiction, biology in no way represents addiction holistically. However, we must begin to see and uncover how the thumb (biomedical) relates to, engages with, and ultimately connects with all the other lenses of addiction study. To do this, we move next to the mind, the psyche, the psychology of addiction, the index finger, or the psychological conceptual lens of addiction.

3

PSYCHOLOGICAL—THE INDEX FINGER

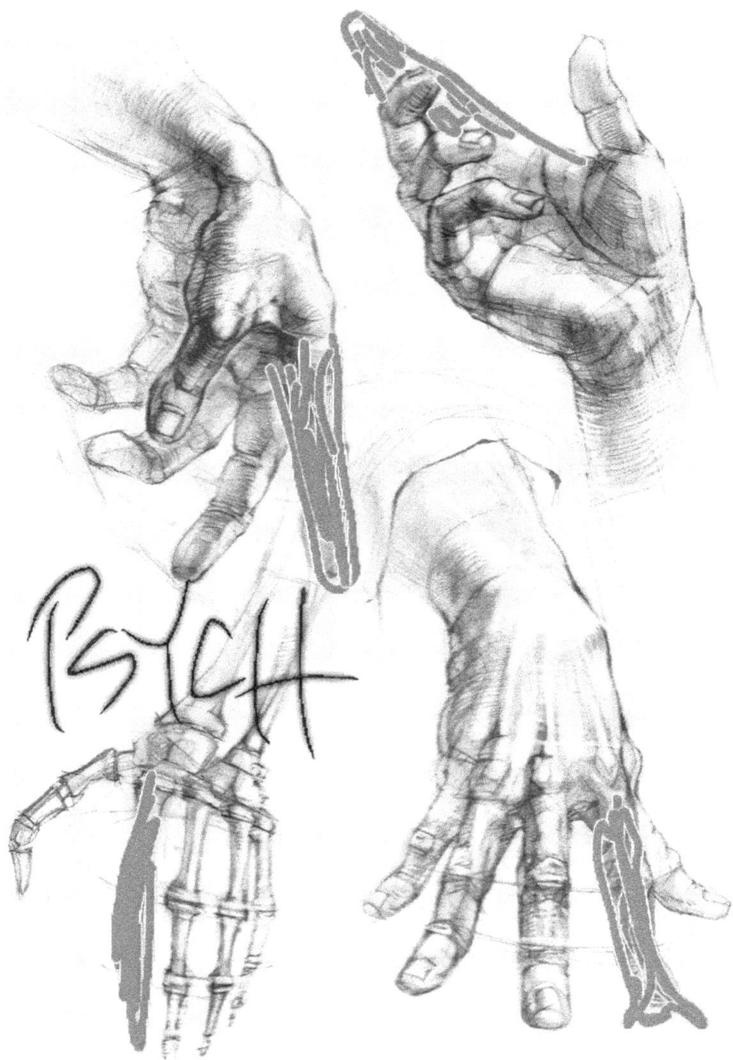

DOI: 10.4324/9781003466321-3

> To all the lost souls living in the realm of hungry ghosts, may you find peace in your heart and soul, and realize drugs will never take away your pain, they will only create more!
>
> —Weston Robins

My Psyche, My Soul, My Breath, My Psychology: ME

The term *psychology* (from the Latinized form of Greek *psykhē* "breath, spirit, soul" (see psyche) + logia "study of" likely emerged in the English language as early as the 17th century.

Its initial meaning was "study of the soul" (see Figure 3.1). The meaning "science or study of the phenomena of the mind" emerged in 1748 in reference to Christian Wolff's (1732/2010) *Psychologia Empirica*. The contemporary

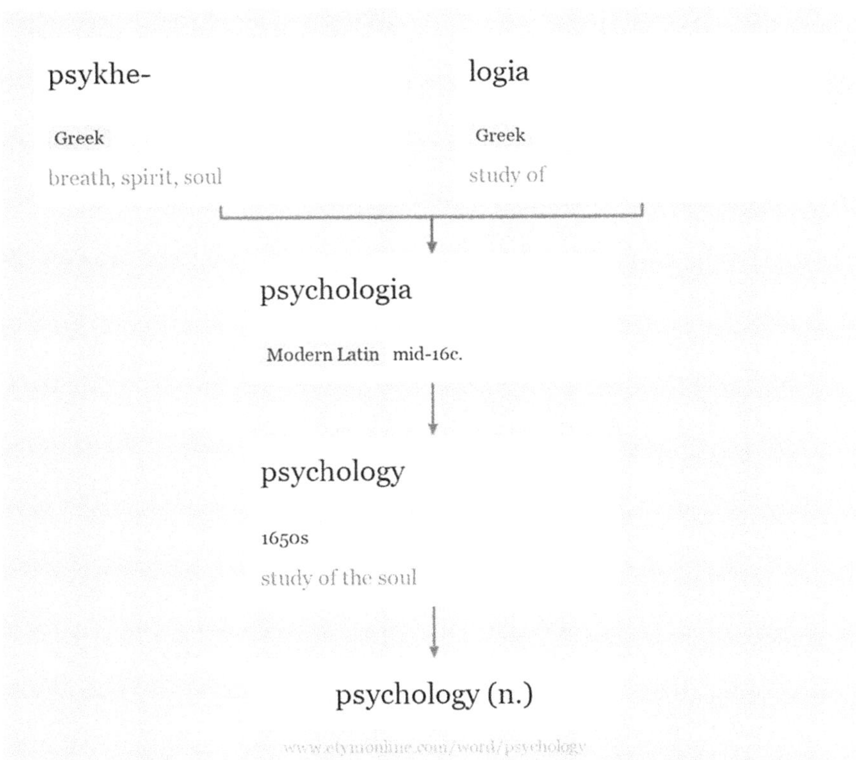

FIGURE 3.1 Definition of Psychology

Note. From "Psychology," Online Etymology Dictionary, 2022 (www.etymonline.com/word/psychology). Copyright 2022 by Douglas Harper.

understanding in the context of behavioral sciences comes from the early 1890s (Online Etymology Dictionary, 2022).

It is important to recognize the growth of language and its impact on the understanding of concepts and terms. Individual terms, such as psychology, psyche, biology, and biochemistry, each have their own history of growth and development as well as their definition, origin, and conceptual meaning. Words matter, and how we utilize and define them often, if not always, impact how we think and behave.

Although the study of psychology can be traced back to the very dawn of civilization and the days of animism and an anthropomorphic conceptualization of human behavior and the supernatural, its earliest historical roots lie in Greek philosophy (Cornford, 1955; Hergenhahn, 2005; Murray, 1955/1981). The earliest philosophers (Thales, Anaximander, Heraclitus, Parmenides, Pythagoras, Empedocles, Anaxagoras, and Democritus) all played a role in examining human life and existence and proposed theories for understanding human behavior (Hergenhahn, 2005). The natural explanations of human cognitive experience, as explored by Socrates, Plato, and Aristotle, laid the foundations for modern science, empiricism, positivism, romanticism, existentialism, and eventually the earliest schools of formal psychology. These schools include Titchener's Structuralism, James and Dewey's Functionalism, and Watson's Behaviorism (Hergenhahn, 2005).

While it would be nearly impossible to summarize the entire historical development of psychology in this context, it is vital to name the historical growth of the terminology and its roots of conceptualization. For this project, I focused on a brief overview of psychology history to illustrate the study of addiction in particular. The definition of psychology has changed as the focus of psychology has changed. At various times in history, psychology has been defined as the study of the psyche or the mind, of the spirit, of consciousness, and more recently as the study of, or the science of, behavior (Hergenhahn, 2005). In addition, I utilized psychology as an umbrella term to represent the study of the human mind and behavior and *psyche* to represent a more holistic understanding of mind, all psychic processes conscious and unconscious, and the subject matter of psychoanalysis (Jung, 1969).

My psychology, psyche, cognition, belief system, and spirit were all impacted dramatically by my relationship with and use of marijuana. I initially experimented with cannabis out of curiosity, but as I continued my use, I found myself reaching for marijuana to curb anxiety and uncomfortable or challenging emotions. Like many other marijuana users, I used the substance as a way to escape the recesses of my mind and psyche. Within seconds of smoking marijuana, I could transport my conscious awareness to a new terrain, one where I was filled with curiosity, relaxation, euphoria, and little to no stress or anxiety. Whether food, sex, television, video games, alcohol, or drugs, many foods and behaviors provide us respite from monotony, stress, pain, and discomfort. But at what cost?

I began smoking at the age of 17, and my relationship with marijuana quickly moved from a monthly engagement to a daily ritual. By the age of 19, I vividly remember feeling and believing that I could never feel happy if I didn't have drugs in my life. I found myself locked in a codependent and enmeshed relationship with marijuana that led me to believe that I would not feel inspiration, motivation, or peace in my life unless I had access to cannabis. I was comfortable being high and promptly began to prefer this realm of consciousness to sober awareness. I could not imagine a time when I would not want, crave, or desire marijuana, so I concluded that I was destined to need and use marijuana for the rest of my life.

It has been 15 years since I have used marijuana, and I am happy to say that I no longer desire, crave, or think of using; however, if I were to smoke marijuana again, I do not believe I would become fixated on using or abusing the plant. I have enriched my life and grown to love sober consciousness so much that marijuana has lost its appeal for me. For clarity, I do not view or conceptualize cannabis as an evil addictive entity nor do I believe it is the "healing of the nation." Instead, I think marijuana is a plant that shifts one's consciousness. Moreover, whether or not it has a beneficial or damaging impact depends on an individual's relationship and engagement with the plant, not the plant itself.

From an early age, I was anxious. In both elementary and middle school, I frequently experienced large surges of nervousness, which made me want to get back home to my comfort zone of food and television (perhaps my first real addictions). Addiction psychologists would likely characterize my behavior as a "self-medicating" tactic for managing my anxiety (Blume et al., 2000). Evidently, this is partially accurate. For me, marijuana was a way to escape pain and anxiety; however, it also offered me increased curiosity and unique access to a different kind of reality. At one point, marijuana was medicine, a healing entity that offered me respite from the day-to-day anxiety and suffering I was experiencing, but as I used it more, it created and caused me much more anxiety than it ever alleviated; herein lies the paradox of drug addiction (Riley, 2011). Marijuana had initially offered respite and a portal toward growth and expansion, or so it seemed, but as my use and abuse progressed, my world quickly shrank, leading me to yearn for escape. My lived experience, my thoughts, my emotions, and my being were all intertwined with my use of substances. There was not one facet of my psyche, my soul, my breath, or my psychology that went untouched by my use.

As we endeavor to move into a deeper examination of the psychological realm of addiction, it is necessary to lay out a brief historical framework of the psychological understanding of addiction. I start this section with psychoanalysis, and this fitting, as psychoanalysis was the first true psychologically focused practice to examine neurosis, malaise, and disorder or disease (Hergenhahn, 2005).

Early Psychoanalytic Approaches to Understanding Addiction

In the earliest days of psychoanalytic development, psychoanalysis was seen as completely separate from medicine and biology. Though both figures in medicine and psychoanalysis would eventually grow to appreciate the relationship between their fields, doctors in the medical field treated the body as a psychochemical machine while psychoanalysts primarily used psychological facts to influence psychological processes. F. Alexander (1948) noted the following:

> Psychoanalysis began to grow and expand and stand on its own with numerous figures focused on understanding the causes of mental illness and using that understanding to help mentally ill patients. After the earliest schools of Psychology: structuralism, functionalism, behaviorism, and Gestalt psychology (Hergenhahn, 2005), Psychoanalysis was finding a strong footing in the field of psychology.
>
> *(p. 169)*

Radó (1933) pioneered research in psychoanalytic studies of addiction with his study, "The Psychoanalysis of Pharmacothymia." Radó and other psychoanalysts framed addiction as a failed and ultimately destructive attempt toward adaptation. In his study, "On the Aetiology of Drug-Addiction," Glover (1932) observed that addicts often use drugs to suppress particular impulses. The work of Radó and Glover formed the basis for the relationships between ego psychology and addiction (Yalisove, 1997).

Over the next three decades, psychoanalysis and ego psychology would influence the study and treatment of addiction in numerous ways. Institutions such as the Menninger Clinic, the Chicago School, and Cambridge Hospital implemented and employed psychoanalytic treatment approaches to working with addiction. By the mid-1900s, addiction treatment in the field of psychology had become increasingly specialized. Due to what psychologists described as poor prognosis and poor motivation, many addicts were discouraged from entering mental health hospitals and outpatient treatment programs in the 1940s and 1950s (Yalisove, 1997). Throughout the 1950s, psychoanalysts such as Claude L. Brown and James Gustafson examined the roles of transference and countertransference in working specifically with addicts, ultimately concluding that traditional psychoanalytic approaches worked well in treating them. Psychotherapists Morris E. Chafetz and Austin Silber held competing views but recommended a dramatic modification when treating addicts (Yalisove, 1997).

In the 1960s and 1970s, community psychiatrists, psychologists, and psychoanalysts framed addiction in the ego structure (Yalisove, 1997). Examining addicts from a standpoint of ego deficits (i.e., early childhood growth and the failure to internalize parental functions), psychoanalytic ego psychologists believed it would be difficult or impossible for addicts to tolerate the rigors of psychoanalytic therapy (Gustafson, 1976; Krystal, 1978; Wurmser, 1974; Yalisove, 1997). This understanding of ego and addiction resulted in other modalities of treatment and approaches.

In the 1970s, some communities opened specialized drug addiction treatment centers, and many of these programs were staffed by individuals in recovery. Medically supervised inpatient detoxification, inpatient rehabilitation programs, and outpatient treatments have continued to expand, and these programs currently and primarily focus on toxicology testing and abstinence from all psychoactive substances. Consequently, there is a growing division between practitioners of these treatment modalities that are similar to the divisions in addiction research. Yalisove (1997) wrote, "Certainly addiction is the perfect vehicle to consider the cultural, social, spiritual, and adaptive as well as psychodynamic and biological factors in the causation of a syndrome" (p. 2). However, the majority of the study and treatment of addiction throughout history has remained divided, with subfields vying for dominance without much opposition or challenge.

Ego psychologists were proposing to be able to define the true nature of addiction, similar to the biomedical community leaning heavily on the physiological disease concept, each specialty field pinpointing one myopic component of addiction and honing in on it as if it were the totality of the phenomena. The thumb (biomedical) and the index finger (psychological) had grown stronger but begun to lose their grip upon the evolutionary growth origins that meant they were units of the same organic structure (the hand).

In many ways, the psychoanalytic—and later psychodynamic—lenses of addiction merely perpetuated more severing and segmenting of addiction. Again, psychoanalytic theory looks to define, examine, and uncover root causes of addiction linked to unconscious impulses and repressed emotions and thoughts, however, it fails to ever break free from imitation and tracing.

Both modern humanistic psychology (Maslow, 1965; Rogers, 1959; Watts, 1951) and existential psychology (Frankl, 1946; May, 1961; Sartre, 1945/2007; Yalom, 1980) were protest responses to behaviorism and psychoanalysis. These movements provided therapists and their patients with a more holistic understanding of human behavior and resulted in a more robust understanding of behaviorism and psychoanalysis. Yet the work of Deleuze and Guattari (1980/1987) and antipsychiatrist R.D. Laing (1971) gave us the language and the tool kit to examine and map addiction through a divergent lens of critique and curiosity.

In the antipsychiatry movement, key radical figures—such as Laing, Cooper, Esterson, Redler, Schatzman, and Berke—questioned the very basis of psychiatry itself: its purpose, its foundational conception of mental illness, and the distinction between madness and sanity itself (Crossley, 1998; Tantam, 1991). It is with this same spirit that I embarked on this project, just as antipsychiatry was interested in the exchange of new ideas, developing new projects, and giving birth to new ways of thinking and acting, I seek to open spaces to better map the movement of addiction and understand it.

One Wolf of Many?

Deleuze and Guattari (1980/1987) used creative ecological analogies to conceptualize addiction. They revealed, for example, that psychoanalysts have organized much of their thought and theory in arborescent or tree-like hierarchical structures. These hierarchies within psychoanalysis have prevented many therapists from seeing larger connections and patterns in the human psyche.

In Deleuze and Guattari's (1987) discussion of deterritorialization, the authors describe lines of flight that serve as openings or windows/portals and that provide individuals a pathway out of the dominant structured majority culture. Lorraine (2005) stated, "A 'line of flight' is a path of mutation precipitated through the actualisation of connections among bodies that were previously only implicit (or 'virtual') that releases new powers in capacities of those bodies to act and respond" (p. 147). To better understand lines of flight, it is also crucial to understand how Deleuze and Guattari view things or concepts.

Deleuze and Guattari preferred to view concepts and phenomena as assemblages and multiplicities, meaning they examine how things connect and interact with one another to create and form new and never-ending mutations. Rather than viewing addiction as a stagnate entity, we can use Deleuze and Guattari's example to understand and conceptualize addiction as an assemblage or multiplicity. Assemblages are organized according to three types of lines that shape their interactions: molar lines (or lines that form a binary and arborescent system of segments), molecular lines (or lines that are still segmentary but more fluid), and lines of flight that rupture the other two lines (Lorraine, 2005, p. 147). For many users, addiction and drugs may initially appear as a true line of flight, but they can quickly become segmentary and eventually stagnant.

> Instead of holes in the world allowing the world lines themselves to run off, the lines of flight coil and start to swirl into black holes; to each addict a hole, group or individual, like a snail. Down instead of high. The molecular microperceptions are overlaid in advance, depending on the drug, by hallucinations, delusions, false perceptions, phantasies, or paranoid

> outbursts. . . . Instead of making a body without organs sufficiently rich or full for the passage of intensities . . . the casual line, creative line, or line of flight immediately turns into a line of death and abolition. . . . Black holes and lines of death.
>
> *(Deleuze & Guattari, 1980/1987, p. 285)*

Deleuze and Guattari accurately describe my lived experience of drug use and eventual habitual drug abuse. My initial substance use felt like a breakthrough, a new frontier, a pathway on a journey to expansion, and an opening to new potential. However, this initial experience quickly became a dark space of confined and repetitious torture.

Deleuze and Guattari's articulation and conceptualization of addiction as an assemblage and drug use as a false line of flight ring true with both my lived experiences of use and the experiences of the clients and families with whom I work. I propose addiction itself is a multiplicity, offering the possibility of a true line of flight, whereas repetitive drug abuse will always collapse the line of flight into rigid stagnation and molar stratification. Moving forward, the distinction between addiction and repetitive substance/drug use will become clearer.

Although I experienced both challenges and anxiety in my childhood, I was fortunate to have a fantastic family and upbringing. I never experienced any abuse, neglect, or severe trauma in my early developmental years, and I came from a two-parent household with a loving, engaged mother and father and an incredible little sister. In my childhood, however, my parents argued and fought frequently. While the fighting never became physical, it was consistent throughout my middle school years. In evaluations of my later addiction, psychodynamic and psychologically inclined therapists might have attributed my addiction to trauma, anxiety, and pain, and, while these factors could certainly have contributed to my drug use, I believe there were instead multiple variables at play.

In their work *Anti-Oedipus*, Deleuze and Guattari (1972) directly challenge such psychological origin stories, raising the question: *One wolf or many?* In the work, the authors challenge psychoanalysis, specifically Freud's singular and simplified view of the unconscious. They utilize the case of Sergei Pankejeff (the wolfman), a famous patient of Freud's, to reframe the unconscious as a platform for multiplicity. Analyzing one of the wolfman's dreams, Freud saw the multiple wolves in the patient's dream as symbols of a singular threat of paternal castration. Deleuze and Guattari, however, were adamantly opposed to this singular interpretation of the wolves and felt all of psychoanalysis continued to refine and ultimately shrink the multiplicity to a unity that was mainly oedipal in nature.

By viewing addiction as a multiplicity, we can break away from traditional psychoanalysis' hierarchical and arborescent conceptualization of addiction as a simplified unity. Deleuze and Guattari view psychoanalytic thought as a singularizing reduction of the multiplicity/complexity, and the lenses of addiction study have similarly reduced the multiplistic nature of addiction to singular origins. My lived experience with addiction however disrupts this reductionism. Just as my biochemistry did not cause and create my addiction, neither did my psychology. Biochemistry and psychology are essential factors, yet neither can stake claim to the etiology of my addiction. To believe that addiction has a root cause is a mistake, a simplification, a castration, and a severing of the multiplicity in addiction studies.

Addiction as a multiplicity operates with bodies without organs (BwOs) and a collective assemblage of enunciations. A BwO is not a single body free of organs; rather, it refers to a cluster of organs deprived of organizations. A body does not necessarily refer to the human body but instead a group or collection without organization. Essentially, BwOs provide an epistemological framework for the nature and structure of organisms. Each organism tends to be categorized and separated in an arborescent and hierarchical manner. However, Deleuze and Guattari (1980/1987) suggested that humanity retains the continual ability to escape these already given logical forms or organizations by becoming a BwO.[1]

In addition, Deleuze and Guattari (1972) challenged psychoanalysis with their concept of the collective assemblage of enunciation through which they assert that there are no singular or individual statements because the statements are always already embedded in the statements of the multiplicity or collective. While Freud yearns to normalize and bring unity to one point, Deleuze and Guattari create and expand psychoanalysis to the multiple, recognizing the unconscious as a multiplicity and attempting to break the arborescent dialect of psyche analysis. These are the tools that allow us to view addiction as a BwO: flowing, fluxing, pulsating, moving, shifting, and always in motion at various speeds.

Addiction is rhizomatic in nature. Substance abuse and habitual drug use are a molar machine—of stagnancy, repetition, and rigidity (black holes and lines of death). Addiction is a flow and flux, jazz improv with no end; habitual substance abuse is a record stuck in a groove and skipping ad nauseam.

Eventually, my use gained momentum and moved from marijuana to include cocaine and methamphetamine: stimulant substances, which increased my anxiety but simultaneously made me feel euphoric and invincible. Feeling anxious yet empowered and capable of anything made the anxiety I was experiencing bearable in many ways. While in the throes of my drug use, my relationship to pain and discomfort began to morph and shift. I now understood that being uncomfortable and feeling challenging emotions were now options rather than necessities. At any moment, I could choose to ingest a substance that could alter, shift, or change every aspect of my present engagement with reality. Whether I was tired, overwhelmed, depressed, or anxious, I could simply lay out white powder, sniff it quickly, and inhale smoke into my lungs, and I would immediately find myself full of energy, awareness, motivation, euphoria, and pleasure. Yet this engagement always came at a price. Whatever euphoria the drugs provided, I inevitably came down from it.

> Instead of making a body without organs sufficiently rich or full for the passage of intensities, drug addicts erect a vitrified or emptied body, or a cancerous one: the causal line, creative line, or line of flight immediately turns into a line of death and abolition.
>
> *(Deleuze & Guattari, 1980/1987, p. 285)*

Habitual drug use is a molar and rigid line, forever closing in on itself and producing an empty BwO. My use was following a line of death. It was a skipping record, a groundhog day of repetitive pattern and habitual stagnation. Though my soul longed to play new frontiers of jazz improvisation, my behaviors were stuck endlessly playing the same note and tone reverberated.[2]

Losing My Soul

I stood on the front step of an apartment complex with a backpack full of personal belongings, including a change of clothes, a portable CD player, two shirts, a toothbrush, and deodorant. The driver who'd brought me to this apartment threw my bag to the curb and left me stranded. I was stuck at the apartment of Boris, a Russian gun enthusiast, whom I visited only when I needed to buy drugs.

At the time, I was using large amounts of cocaine and methamphetamine, so I wasn't surprised when, two friends, Jennifer and Barbara, called me to see if I could help them buy cocaine. They picked me up from a restaurant where I was drinking, and we drove to Boris's house. On the ride to the apartment, we laughed and joked with anticipatory excitement for what the night might have in store once we were high.

Boris answered the apartment door in a black tank top and shorts. Tall and thin, he had a shaved head and squinty eyes with big, dark circles under them. His presence was intimidating, to say the least. As Boris led us to his bedroom, a feeling of unease came over me. I had been to his apartment only once before, and he had been mentally unstable. During my last visit, he had threatened to shoot someone during an argument. But I had good reason to set abandon my safety, logic, and reasoning: I wanted drugs.

As we walked down the hallway and entered the bedroom, I saw that Boris had spread several firearms across his mattress. Boris sat down and proceeded to cut up several lines of cocaine. He offered some to me, which I willingly took. Boris then asked Barbara to sit by him on the bed. He handed Barbara the small mirror plate with several lines of cocaine on it. As she lowered her head and drew her nostril to a little straw to snort the cocaine, Boris forcefully

FIGURE 3.2 My Portrait

grabbed the top of her head with his hand and held it down aggressively. Barbara immediately sat up in fear and shot me a glance that I will never forget. Her eyes seemed to cry: *help*. Boris was obviously unstable and aggressive and his impulsivity had transformed into repulsive sexual energy.

Neither the girls nor I knew how to handle this situation. Customarily, I would have stood up and confronted Boris; but I was all too aware of the arsenal of guns strewn across his bed. In combination with his impulsivity, the guns made me hesitant to make any sudden moves. Jennifer and Barbara remained calm, and within the next ten minutes, they made reasonable excuses to leave; Boris seemed to accept them reluctantly. I left soon after, and as I walked out of Boris's apartment, I felt immediately relieved to get away from a disturbing and potentially violent situation. Arriving at the parking lot, however, Jennifer and Barbara were gone, and what remained was my backpack, which they had thrown to the ground.

This habitual process was exhaustive and often left me feeling lower than I'd felt before I used. I cyclically avoided pain and discomfort with substances, only to experience more pain and discomfort. In my attempt to escape pain and monotony, I was simply creating more of it with my use. The immanent molecular potentiality was failing as all that existed was a molar/rigid and stagnate habituation. As Deleuze and Guattari (1972) described it, the molecular and the line of segmentarity hold the potential to either burst into a line of flight and open new spaces or fold in on themselves and create a molar line of no openings and stuck circular repetition. My drug use at times promised openings and gave me the false sense of a new experience, a new beginning, a new frontier, but over time, I started to understand that there was nothing new, nothing even close to new. I had entered a been there done that space in which so many before me had stagnated, the legion of false heroes moving toward a little death and a long fatigue.

My use was severing lines of flight left and right and suffocating my creative potentiality in a merry-go-round of same shit different day. I didn't just need to stop using substances—I had to make a stopover, to start from the "middle," to bifurcate from the middle. It was more simple in nature than I understood. I didn't need to stop my creativity or exploration; rather, I needed to stop my redundancy, habituation, and monotonous repetition. It is important to remember that the essence and heart of addictive energy is not necessarily negative, rather it is molecular and supple with the potential to transform into lines of flight or lines of death. Always a potentiality, the record can continue to skip, or it can become free from the groove, and the needle can bounce to a new track. My use was stuck, stagnant, and repetitive, and I needed the record to quit skipping if I was ever going to pursue a different line. But how?

My habitual drug use and substance ingestion was the issue, not my addiction. My addiction was the molecular, supple line, ready to transform into a line of creative flight. My drug use was the molar line of rigidity folding in on itself, my addiction was the opening and offshoot potential line of flight that could shift my life in a new direction.

Viewing the index finger as the psychological conceptualization of addiction, we again see how addiction study has continually been striated, compartmentalized, and simplified. If we do not begin to understand addiction as a flow of intensity, a machinic assemblage, and a multiplicity rather than a stagnant, rigid phenomenon, we will continue to repeat a pattern of reterritorialization. The addiction field continues to sabotage itself by naming what addiction is while searching for etiology and oversimplifying a highly complex and nuanced flow of energy. Observing and mapping the ebb and flow of intensities of addiction as opposed to nailing it down and attempting to capture it is my project.

The psychologically myopic understanding of addiction is yet merely another attempt to capture and stratify addiction as a stable concept. G. Bateson's (1979) understanding of the hand as a set of relationships between the fingers allows for an exploration of the spaces in between. Much like his concept of the human hand, the field of addiction study continues to place more attention on the striated and molar fingers without mapping the spaces in between the fingers, nor the relationships between them. The space in between the fingers reveals the rhizomatic nature of addiction flow and energy.

To understand the nature of addiction as rhizomatic we must begin to see the intensities of addiction, to follow the offshoots, to map the chain of connections, to map how addiction moves, breathes, sleeps, eats, and functions as a multiplicity that is always becoming. Also, we must begin to differentiate between addiction and that of habitual molar and rigid drug abuse. Addiction is molecular in the sense that it can either fall upon itself and fold into a rigid/molar segmentarity or could open into a smooth line of flight. However, as stated previously, habitual and repeated drug use will always create a line of death, a molar rigidity, a false line of flight.

At some point, I knew that I had two choices. I could either continue my daily dance with substances, which made me feel resentful, frustrated, more anxious, and more afraid, or break away from my drug use entirely and begin to construct and create a life which would bring me joy and peace in a way that drugs never could. However, I didn't know how to do this and felt lost, hopeless, and defeated. Ultimately, I had to break free, find a path, a light, a way, a crack, a crevice, an opening that would free me from the line of death I was living. Deleuze and Guattari (1980/1987) offered the path and the freedom:

> This is how it should be done: lodge yourself on a stratum, experiment with the opportunities it offers, find an advantageous place on it, find potential movements of deterritorialization, possible lines of flight, experience them, produce flow conjunctions here and there, try out continuums of intensities segment by segment, have a small plot of new land at all times.
>
> *(p. 161)*

I intuitively knew I needed to deterritorialize but had no words or language of articulation to describe what my heart felt. However, I knew that continued and repeated drug use was leading me to a segmentarity all the more rigid, a territorialization all the more artificial. I would never find a true line of flight unless I broke from my pattern of habitual drug use. "The casual line, or the line of flight, of drugs is constantly being segmentarized under the most rigid of forms, that of dependency, the hit and the dose, the dealer" (Deleuze & Guattari, 1980/1987, p. 284). I had to abandon habitual drug use to grow, to seek, to continue becoming, and to expand. My music, art, creation, dreams, visions, and potentiality were all being stifled and suffocated daily. I was no longer becoming, I was slowly shutting down and folding in on myself. If I were to live again, I had to fight to decalcify my behavioral rigidity. If I could move away from drug use, I knew in my heart I could use avenues of addiction and my addictive energy to create and make a life of poetic art. I understood that I could taste life again, experience joy again, play again, and engage in the process of becoming again. Deleuze and Guattari (1980/1987) revealed the path again:

> To reach the point where "to get high or not to get high" is no longer the question, but rather whether drugs have sufficiently changed the general conditions of space and time perception so that nonusers can succeed in passing through the holes in the world and following the lines of flight at the very place where means other than drugs become necessary.
>
> *(p. 286)*

This was my path, my substance use had served me in all the ways it could and now was my moment to pass through spaces already opened and follow new lines of flight to growth and continual becoming. I didn't know exactly where to start, but I did know what to move away from. To move toward becoming, to deterritorialize, to become imperceptible was the path. I would have done anything to break from habituation, stagnation, and the molar line of rigidified territorialities.

Bateson's concept of the hand and seeing the index finger as the psychological lens and segmentarity of addiction, we see how inner lived experience (psychology) and cognitive narratives greatly impact how one views substance use. My understanding of my relationship to substances was beginning to shift. I was beginning to understand that the once open, free and exploratory terrain of my substance use had simply become a closed and myopic space of habituation. Even my cerebral nature had been slowed and stagnated by my habitual use. My psychic headspace was simplified and rigid, focused only on obtaining and using substances. I no longer was thinking rhizomatically, exploratorily, and creatively, as my thoughts and emotions were rigid, structured, predictable, and desperate—fixated on one thing: drug use.

Now, more than ever, it is crucial to understand how these components of addiction interrelate and influence one another to begin to look at them—not as separate—but as concepts that bleed into and interplay with one another in a continual feedback loop. Even experts working from an interdisciplinary and multidisciplinary approach to understanding addiction still view these arenas as separate from one another. Moving beyond these viewpoints and seeing how they overlap, influence/impact, and perpetuate each other is key. G. Bateson (1991) wrote:

> What I'm saying is that the world into which we are moving, the world in whose terms we have to think, is a world of patterns, and in that world, there are tautologies and logics which we can use for explaining, for building accurate language and for creating some rigor. It's not like the language of quantities and such things. It's a language of patterns and, for most of us, an unfamiliar business.
>
> *(pp. 180, 184)*

G. Bateson (1991) wanted experts to recognize that everything is connected and that we must learn to organize the language of the mind around a new epistemology to understand the world through patterns, relationships, differences, and interfaces. Once we recognize the grand interconnectedness, we can begin to understand ourselves and the world we co-create.

The goal of my project is to demonstrate a new epistemology and a new understanding of addiction. As I continue to map the scaffolding of addiction, I continue to raise G. Bateson's (1979, p. 8) exploratory question: "What is the pattern that connects?" Whether we look through the biomedical, physiological, neurological, psychological, or humanistic lens of addiction studies, we must ask ourselves: What is the pattern that connects? What are the relationships between the lenses? We must begin to think in terms of an ecology of mind, seeing the totality or patterns of relations between organisms and their environments (N. Bateson, 2016, p. 20). We must also begin to see transcontextually (N. Bateson, 2016, p. 79) to move increasingly to the patterns and relationships of systems and away from disciplines and fields as separate entities. N. Bateson (2016) stated the following:

> I am giving up on interdisciplinarity, transdisciplinarity, and even metadisciplinairity. The world is not made of disciplines. I still hold the work of my academic colleagues in high esteem, but I no longer place the academy at the center of the solar system of knowledge. I now see the academic contribution to learning as one aspect of knowledge—among many. Life is not divisible into the departments of a university, nor is our understanding of life greatly increased by standard research practices, which tend to pull their "subject" matter out of the larger contexts they exist in, to facilitate focused study. The studied subjects never get put back into their relationships, and the contexts never seem to be describable in the data.
>
> *(p. 79)*

Academic disciplines' inability to fully see and examine relational webbed connections continues to push us to fight for a transcontextual framework of study and a better understanding of the interdependency that characterizes living (and arguably nonliving) systems (N. Bateson, 2016, p. 79).

Transcontextuality and autoethnography allow me to share my lived experience of addiction and also integrate it within the study of addiction. Taking time to peer through each lens and discipline of study to reveal the patterns that connect. For I have experienced addiction fully, now what does my story reveal about addiction theory and study as a whole? How can my lived experience better serve as an entry point into understanding the complex rhizomatic and multiplistic nature of addiction? My story is deeply personal and idiosyncratic, laced with haecceity, yet simultaneously it is the story I share with so many other people. It is perhaps even the story of the whole of human experience—pain and suffering, joy and pleasure, creation, and destruction—the hero's journey.

In addition, the clients, families, and communities I serve are transcontextual, each with their own voice, separate and unique, yet all connected to one another in the ecological web of human existence. Before all else, we are ecosystems, I am complex, I am a dream, and I am an ecology of selves (N. Bateson, 2016, p. 28). To understand addiction, we must understand all of the relational and transcontextual patterns that connect us to ourselves and to one another. However, before we delve more deeply into the interconnected ecological webbing of addiction, let us move to the third finger on the hand of addiction, the sociocultural.

Notes

1 https://photos.app.goo.gl/nz8NemBMVLWiPGky7
2 https://photos.app.goo.gl/4azGf7iBAiimbgqaA

4

SOCIOCULTURAL—THE MIDDLE FINGER

DOI: 10.4324/9781003466321-4

Addiction: Language Matters

Although the concept of addiction has emerged throughout history, it was not until the mid-20th century that the idea of *addiction* began to encompass all socially unacceptable uses of alcohol and drugs. B. Alexander (2008) detailed the history of the word, explaining that, prior to the mid-19th century, addiction had a simpler definition that was similar to the ancient use of the Latin noun *addictionem* and the verb *addicere*. The traditional English definition appeared in the first fascicule of the authoritative dictionary of the English language, the *Oxford English Dictionary*, published in 1884. It reappeared, essentially unchanged in all subsequent editions. A different definition (addiction) eventually grew out of the traditional definition, and though it first appeared in the 1933 *Supplement* to the Dictionary, it was not added to the main text until 1989. The traditional definition from 1884 reads:

> Addiction . . . [ad. L. addiction-em, n. Of action f. Addic-ere; see ADDICT.] *Rom. Law*. A formal giving over or delivery by sentence of court. Hence, a surrender, or dedication, of any one to a master. The state of being (self-) addicted or giving *to a* habit or pursuit; devotion.
>
> *(p. 28)*

In *The Globalization of Addiction*, B. Alexander (2008) traced changes to the language of substance abuse throughout Western history to examine how the meaning of the word "addiction"—only used to talk about alcohol abuse—grew to encompass all substance abuse (opium, cocaine, heroin, marijuana, LSD, barbiturates, amphetamine, ecstasy, and methamphetamine) by the end of the 19th century.

The definition, usage, and meaning of the term addiction continued to evolve. From the 20th to the 21st century, authorities on substance abuse have continually debated and failed to agree on a comprehensive definition of addiction. Leadership over both the *Diagnostic and Statistical Manual of Mental Disorders* (DSM) and the *International Classification of Diseases* (ICD)—the main resources for the classification of mental diseases—have tried to expunge the word "addiction" from scholarly discourse, replacing it with "substance dependence," "substance abuse," and "dependence syndrome." These replacement terms have joined the semantic clutter in the labyrinth because their definitions are not clear enough and because cultural differences make it difficult for experts to agree on what kinds of drug use are problematic (B. Alexander, 2008).

To help organize this semantic clutter, B. Alexander (2008) eventually presented four contemporary ways of understanding the word "addiction," as derived from its traditional definition:

Addiction[1]: Overwhelming involvement with drugs or alcohol that is harmful to the addicted person, to society, or to both.

Addiction^{2}*:* Encompasses addiction^{1} and non-overwhelming involvements with drugs or alcohol that are problematic to the addicted person, society, or both.
Addiction^{3}*:* Overwhelming involvement with any pursuit whatsoever (including, but not limited to, drugs or alcohol) that is harmful to the addicted person, to society, or to both.
Addiction^{4}*:* Overwhelming involvement with any pursuit whatsoever that is not harmful to the addicted person or to society.

These delineations, although useful in creating more clarity about the nuances of addiction, also add confusion to an already complicated arena of study. Moreover, most individuals continue to view addiction as a negative (based on *Addiction*^{1}*–Addiction*^{3}), and the term itself rarely if ever has positive connotations (*Addiction*^{4}).

To better understand the movement and flow of addiction, we must look to examine how our culture and society have defined, understood, treated, and lived with addiction. Most importantly we must ask ourselves why we continue to try and define and encapsulate addiction when this has done little to advance the field or help individuals under our therapeutic care. We must also begin to map the vastness of what we have called "addiction," which is, ultimately, an ever-moving, ever-growing, ever-changing entity in flux—or as Deleuze and Guattari (1980/1987) would put it, a multiplicity. As a society, we have tried to pin down and define addiction, and now it is time for us to expand our understanding of addiction. If we are ever to keep up with the nature of addiction itself, we must not merely define it but rather observe how it moves and grows throughout time, throughout space, throughout culture, and throughout our collective society at large.

Cultural and Societal Impact

None of us exist in isolation. We are always surrounded by a particular geographical environment, culture, and social milieu. Throughout the history of formal psychology, researchers in every school of thought (structuralism, functionalism, psychodynamic, behaviorism, and cognitive) have placed emphasis on the behavior of the individual (Stangor & Walinga, 2014). Although the first official social psychology studies began in the early 1900s (Triplett, 1898) and the first texts were published in 1908 (McDougall, 1908/2003; Ross, 1908/1974), many people in the field of psychology were still heavily focused on individual neurosis or malaise. As the decades went by, various psychologists with different social interests began to place more emphasis on the impact of society, culture, and the social rather than on individual behavior. These figures and arenas of focus included experimental social psychology (Festinger, 1954), studies of conformity (Asch, 1952; Sherif, 1936), and studies of obedience (Haney et al., 1973; Milgram, 1974; Stangor & Walinga, 2014).

Social psychology began to grow and develop as a broader field of study with arenas of focus such as helping others (Darley & Latane, 1968), human aggression (Berkowitz, 1974), group behavior (Janis, 1972), and models of persuasion/advertising (Eagly & Chaiken, 1993; Hovland et al., 1963). Currently, social psychology is growing and expanding in various arenas of study to determine how the social impacts and influences the individual and vice versa. What continues to be clear, however, is the separation and severing from the study of social psychology and the study of individual psychology. Although some researchers have explored the overlap and relationship between these arenas, we once again begin to see separate and compartmentalized areas of study and practice.

As we continue this project, let us move to the middle finger or the sociocultural arenas and lenses of addiction. Mapping the hand of addiction, it again is important and critical to restate the specific goals of my project. I wish not to further sever the fingers/arenas on the hand of addiction but rather to examine, explore, and cartograph the relationship between the fingers and the ways they are intrinsically woven together in a tapestry of threads that cannot exist in separation from one another. N. Bateson (2016) noted the following:

> I am not only what is in my body, I am also my personality, my culture, my emotions, my spirit. Finding where exactly the outside world ends and I begin—is not so easy. My culture influences so much: My ideas, my language, my eating habits, my music, my clothing, my education. And somehow, under closer scrutiny, none of those things has a clear root either. Languages are compiled across time and movements of people, as are recipes, and religious traditions. Even plants and animals move around the globe.
>
> *(p. 19)*

It is this inability to define where the "I" begins and ends and where the "We" exist. We never exist in isolation, therefore we are always immersed in the engagement with the social other and the cultural influences at large. Like a recursive feedback loop, the echo of a snare drum, a reverberation of a scream, any noise, presence, or existence of a thing impacts the world around it and vice versa.

As we move through the hand of addiction, thumb (biological), index finger (psychological), we arrive at the middle finger (sociocultural). It is vital to review and examine the sociological and collective influences and impacts on addiction. As mentioned in the previous chapter, much of psychology's history has placed attention on the individual's solipsistic struggles with addiction (Nathan et al., 2016), leaving little room for a broader social understanding of addiction.

Using the language of ailments, allergies, ego, psyche, and emotions, the field of psychology has disproportionately defined addiction as an individual malaise or neurosis. As we begin to examine the sociocultural lens of addiction, we will gain a better understanding of how addiction arises in communities and how the collective understanding of addiction impacts every facet of how it moves, flows, and fluxes. One could say that this entire project is an attempt to open, expand, and carve out a new collective understanding of addiction as a whole. Not an understanding that attempts to define, capture, or pin down addiction as a stagnate entity but rather a revealing and unveiling of how addiction temporospatially shapeshifts on the plane of immanence.

It is important that a brief history is given to not only the field of study of social psychology but also to the history of substance use and psychoactive mind-altered states from a sociological and cultural lineage perspective. The history of substances and drug use, drug policy, and drug legislation and treatment from a sociocultural perspective is extensive, so I provide only a brief overview of that perspective for the purposes of this project. Now, we will dive into the sociocultural lenses to better understand the wholeness of addiction.

Earliest Usage of Psychoactive Substances

Throughout human history, psychoactive plants have been utilized to shift and alter states of consciousness (Crocq, 2007). Many cultures have used various plants to engage in ritualistic, spiritual, and religious ceremonies. Sayin (2014), who is an expert in neuro/psychopharmacology and forensic sciences, traced the wide range of substance use in shaman and pagan subcultures in detail. These subcultures include the following: African native religions; Witi cult; South American native religions; Amazon Cultures; Central American Cultures; Mexican subcultures; Aztec, Maya, and Inca; Wiccan and witch subcultures; Satanists; American Indians; Greek and Hellenistic cultures; Sufis; Hassan Sabbah's Hashissins; Hindu, Indian and Tibetan cultures; and some of the Nordic subcultures.

Sayin (2014) listed the psychoactive ingredients of the plants these subcultures used during religious rituals, including the narcotic analgesics (opium), THC (cannabis), psilocybin (magic mushrooms), mescaline (peyote), ibogaine (Tabernanthe iboga), DMT (Ayahuasca and phalaris species), Peganum harmala, bufotenin, muscimol (Amanita muscaria), thujone (absinthe, Arthemisia absinthium), ephedra, mandragora, star lotus, and Salvia divinorum.

Although many cultures have engaged with substances throughout history, they almost always used them with purpose, intention, respect, and reverence aiming toward transcendence and spiritual development. However, these cultures never conceptualized the experience of working with substances as addiction. Individuals in these cultures never abused or used substances compulsively, and rarely did persons or communities experience negative consequences related to their use (Vetulani, 2001). As we will later see, it was not until the emergence of Western culture and individualism that the concepts of substance abuse and addiction began to take hold and influence many people.

In the 1800s, America had little to no understanding of addiction, as most people used substances medicinally. By the 1900s, international trade and exchange resulted in a surge in drug usage. Local and state legislators launched multiple antidrug campaigns and passed antidrug laws as the body of literature about addiction expanded. These factors would be the catalyst for the eventual prohibition of alcohol, tobacco, and the nonmedical use of opiates and cocaine (White, 2004).

Many factors, including psychosocial disintegration, systemic racism, and legal and political variables, began to accelerate drug and substance abuse (White, 2010). William White has conducted the most extensive and in-depth research on addiction in the United States (williamwhitepapers.com). White has written hundreds of articles, books, and chapters on addiction, tracing detailed timelines and chronologies of happenings throughout addiction history. In his primary work, *Slaying the Dragon: The History of Addiction Treatment and Recovery in America*, White details the entire history of addiction in Western civilization, from the origins of addiction, drug policy, and legislation to the history of drug treatment to the modern-day current field of addiction studies. The text has been organized both chronologically and thematically and is beyond thorough. Rather than replicate or repeat any of White's work, I wish to highlight pivotal and important moments of addiction's history in American Western civilization with particular emphasis on the sociocultural to illustrate the profound impact collective culture has on the manifestation of addiction.

Western Prohibition and Legislation: A Brief History

In the 1800s, doctors throughout the United States began to use substances for medicinal purposes. A German chemist, F.W.A. Sertürner, first discovered morphine in 1804, and its use rapidly increased after the advent of the hypodermic needle in the 1870s. In England, a chemist synthesized heroin from morphine in 1874, and it gained more prominence after Bayer utilized it in cough suppressant medicine in 1898. With the support of Freud and the United States Army, the medical community began to use cocaine in various tonics, ointments, and sprays between 1890 and 1905 (King County Bar Association [KCBA], 2005).

Throughout the early 1900s, these primary substances were on the rise as treatments for various maladies and ailments. Heroin was used to treat respiratory illnesses, cocaine was used in products such as Coca-Cola, and physicians regularly prescribed patients morphine for pain relief. Additionally, many people advertised and used marijuana, opium, morphine, heroin, and cocaine medicinally.

By the 20th century, US policymakers had begun to witness more abusive and habitual use of these substances, and the temperance movement arose in an attempt to counteract this (White, 2014). While the use of different drugs was both legal and widespread in 19th-century United States, many American institutions advised people against the use of drugs. Doctors, religious leaders, and government officials warned communities against excessive substance use and, as proponents of prohibition began to gain political traction, they advocated for moderation or restriction. Meanwhile, social and economic upheavals helped bring the issue to mainstream America (KCBA, 2005).

Although leaders in the temperance movement and prohibition sought to control substance use, their advocacy was marred by covert political, social, cultural, and moral agendas. Religiosity and social and political ideals began to shape the conceptualization, treatment, and legislation of substance use throughout the United States (KCBA, 2005; White, 2004). The United States was beginning to utilize drug policies and procedures as a cover for the institutionalization of certain morals and values, immigration policy, race relations, and economic growth. This practice of using drug policy and legislation as a means of advancing other well-defined political and social agendas would characterize much of the history surrounding substance use even up to the current day. Moreover, while prohibition's leaders promised to eradicate poverty, crime, illness, violence, and debt through the control of substance use, their work ultimately increased and intensified these social inequities (White, 2014).

Based on this cultural experience, it is clear that the prohibition of substances has neither stopped nor slowed down substance abuse but has instead contributed to a plethora of negative sociocultural effects. Richard Branson (2012) quoted H.L. Mencken's 1925 essay:

> Prohibition has not only failed in its promises but actually created additional serious and disturbing social problems throughout society. There is not less drunkenness in the Republic but more. There is not less crime, but more. . . . The cost of government is not smaller, but vastly greater. Respect for the law has not increased but diminished.
>
> *(para. 1)*

In 1914, Congress passed the Harrison Anti-Narcotic Act. This act restricted the use of opiates and cocaine to legitimate medical purposes. Now, it was up to physicians to regulate the use of these substances (White, 2014). This period of drug criminalization has had a long-lasting and lingering impact on those struggling with addiction in the United States. White (2014) explained that doctors who treated addicts were at extreme risk and could lose their medical practice through arbitrary interpretations of "good faith" and "proper treatment." As a result of this policy, "More than 25,000 physicians were indicted under the Harrison Act between 1914 and 1938. Some 3,000 actually went to jail, while another 20,000 paid substantial fines" (White, 2014, p. 152). Soon, physicians simply stopped treating addicts to protect themselves from liability. This deficit in the medical community meant that individuals had to seek and obtain these substances on their own.

Coyne and Hall (2017) outlined in detail the negative ramifications of prohibition. Alcohol prohibition backfired completely and was a failure on all fronts. Alcohol consumption rose upwards of 70%, the quality of the product was varied and put people at risk for overdoses and alcohol poisoning, and many former alcohol users began consuming more opium, cocaine, and illegal substances. Meanwhile, crime and corruption increased and flourished (Coyne & Hall, 2017, p. 2). The evidence was clear: prohibition was only exacerbating the dilemma of drug and alcohol addiction; it did absolutely nothing to slow down individual use and contributed to increased use of other drugs.

Over the next several years, the United States put multiple laws, drug policies, and procedures in place that impacted and influenced the country's sociocultural understanding of addiction. These laws included: The Porter Act of 1930, The Marijuana Tax Act of 1937, The Boggs Act of 1951, The Narcotic Control Act of 1956, and the Drug Abuse Control Act of 1965. These laws would ultimately lead up to the war on drugs.

These drug policies and procedures began to set the stage for the reform movements of the 1960s and 1970s. Drug use and abuse were in flux, and the country was trying to mediate, control, and contain substances and their use via several platforms. The overarching sentiment across the country, however, was that drugs are highly addictive and damaging and had the potential to destroy communities and individuals; as a result of these beliefs, most Americans believed communities needed to put harsher penalties in place for drug use and abuse.

The Real War on Drugs/Just Say No

When I was visiting my parents a few years ago, my mom found an old VHS tape and randomly put it in the VCR. In the video, I saw myself at six years old, performing comedy skits with my dad. At one point in the skit, I said, "Come on, Dad, let's sing a song about drugs. Drugs are bad, never do drugs, just say no, cause they're all around." As I watched this video, I felt haunted by what I recognized as a foreshadowing of what would later occur in my adolescence and young adulthood.

My earliest memories of learning about drugs were from a class project I conducted in fifth grade. The "Just Say No" drug campaign and the war on drugs of the 1980s were in full effect. Our elementary school teacher required students to use a large white sheet of poster board, the standard for nearly every school activity at the time, to creatively and artistically depict the multitude of dangers and harm that drugs have on individuals. I vaguely remember using different colored markers to sketch a syringe, a crack pipe, a marijuana joint, and lines of cocaine. Off to the side of the pictures were the words and phrases: "Just Say No," "Crack is Wack," "Drugs are for Losers," and "Drugs Kill."

Earlier that week, our school held an assembly where law enforcement displayed real drug samples and then proceeded to explain in detail the extreme dangers and damaging effects of these substances. The presentation worked; I was terrified! I remember coming home in tears and in a panic crying to my mom that I was afraid the "drugs were going to get me." My mom reassured me that drugs could not get me unless I decided to use them. This statement came as a tremendous relief. I was safe; the drugs were not going to appear and force themselves on me. I just needed to stay away from them. In my 8-year-old mind, I could not understand how anyone would ever decide to use these horrible, life-damaging substances. I was baffled that anyone would willingly and consciously choose to engage with a substance that was guaranteed to cause only harm and damage to them. Only later would I discover the rich complexity of paradoxes that exist in the world of drug use and addiction.

In 1971, President Richard Nixon held a press conference, saying, "America's public enemy number one in the United States is drug abuse. In order to fight and defeat this enemy, it is necessary to wage a new, all-out offensive" (Nixon, 1971, para. 3). While government officials would present the war on drugs as a campaign to end the negative impact of drugs on families, communities, and individuals, the domino effect of legislation, imprisonment, and new policies ultimately wreaked havoc on impoverished communities and the nation at large.

To examine and explore the sociopolitical ramifications of the war on drugs, I would need much more than one chapter. Entire canons of work have been devoted to the sociopolitical aspects and details of drug law, policy, and legislation. Although it is massively important work, this is not my current project, and I will only be able to break the surface of this history as I continue to deterritorialize the hand of addiction.

In her work, *The New Jim Crow*, M. Alexander (2010), traced incarceration rates and revealed the horrifying results of the war on drugs. She examined how mass incarceration had impacted low socioeconomic status communities and how it had both overtly and covertly preserved and perpetuated racial segregation. M. Alexander (2010) wrote:

> The impact of the drug war has been astounding. In less than 30 years, the U.S. penal population exploded from around 300,000 to more than

2 million, with drug convictions accounting for the majority of the increase. The United States now has the highest rate of incarceration in the world, dwarfing the rates of nearly every developed country, even surpassing those in highly repressive regimes like Russia, China, and Iran. In Germany, 93 people are in prison for every 100,000 adults and children. In the United States, the rate is roughly eight times that, or 750 per 100,000.

(p. 6)

This increase in incarceration has done little to slow down drug and substance use and abuse. Researchers have evaluated the flaws in the methodological etiology of the war on drugs and explored and explained in depth its negative impact on communities (B. Alexander, 2008; M. Alexander, 2010; Hari, 2015). Numerous antidrug campaigns, policies, and legislation, for example, have been directly linked to both overt and covert systemic racism and prejudice toward minority groups. As White (2004) explained:

> There were many influences that have shaped the anti-drug campaigns, but one glaring theme is the association of particular drugs with specific minority groups. The West Coast anti-opium campaign of the 1870s linked opium to the Chinese during a period of intense racial and class conflict. The first anti-cocaine laws in the South linked cocaine with violence by blacks at a time there is little evidence of widespread cocaine use among African Americans. This history continued: the drive toward alcohol prohibition tapped anti-Catholic and anti-German sentiment, the anti-heroin campaign tapped growing fears about crime and violence by immigrant youth, the anti-cannabis campaign heavily targeted Mexican immigrants, and the anti-cocaine laws of the 1980s were targeted primarily against poor communities of color.
>
> *(p. 94)*

Repeatedly, we see that drug laws and policy have rarely ever truly been about a war on drugs. Rather, it has been a war on people, communities, families, and cultures. As antidrug campaigns promised to reduce crime, poverty, and violence by eliminating drugs from our culture, they exacerbated all the aforementioned problems by tearing apart communities and incarcerating sick and impoverished individuals. Meanwhile, institutions, legal systems, privatized prisons, and political parties all economically benefited from this war.

The basic premise of the war on drugs was to eradicate drugs from society altogether; more simply, the mission: "no drugs=no problems." This approach to eradicating drugs is erroneous in and of itself. There has never been a time when human beings have not used substances to change consciousness, and it is naïve to believe that we will ever live in a world free of mind-altering substances. Each day, as technology grows exponentially, we are creating new synthetic formations of substances, and this will likely continue directly alongside the advancement of technology.

Even when substances are scarce, people develop and practice organic forms of changing consciousness and their perception of reality (via transcendental meditation, holotropic breathwork, and fasting). Changing consciousness and using substances are foundational to our humanity; much like the drives of hunger, thirst, and sex, we are all driven to shift our conscious engagement with reality (Cardeña & Winkelman, 2011). Whether we alter our experience of consciousness by riding a roller coaster, hanging upside down, dancing until we fall into a trance, or spinning around until we get dizzy, we all seek out and desire altered states of consciousness and have experimented with consciousness-shifting practices for centuries (Cardeña & Winkelman, 2011).

It is important to remember that the war on drugs is layered with intentional and systemic racism of marginalized communities. The CIA intentionally flooded the black community with heroin during and after the Vietnam war, early opium laws correlated with increasing Chinese immigration, marijuana propaganda correlated with increasing Mexican immigration, and the government produced the crack cocaine epidemic of the 1980s (Hart, 2013). The more we look into drug policy, history, and treatment, the better we understand the relationship between these policies and political and economic agendas.

Although it is easy to blame society and culture for creating, perpetuating, and exacerbating addiction and drug use in particular, we must always be careful not to replicate the follies of the field of addiction studies by looking for a particular scapegoat (individual biological, psychological, sociocultural), for there is not one factor alone that produces addiction. Rather, addiction is an organism that grows differently in different environments, both internally and externally. It is more important to understand and examine these environments and watch closely the way in which addiction moves, so that we may better understand its nature. Again, our goal is to increase our understanding of addiction, not to play detective and catch addiction in the act; we already know addiction will always strike and we can never eradicate it. We must instead ask ourselves how can we observe it, influence it, shape, and shift it and learn more about its possibilities and potentialities.

Moving into the late 20th century, the collective narrative was that morphine, heroin, cocaine, and crack kill and are the most addictive drugs known to man (White, 2004). However, two works in particular, Alexander et al.'s (1981) Rat Park study and Robins et al.'s (1974) Vietnam Addiction study, would begin to directly challenge this narrative head-on.

Rat Park and Vietnam

In their Rat Park study, Alexander et al. (1981) studied how community influenced the oral ingestion of morphine in rat populations. In previous studies, rats in isolation consistently chose water laced with cocaine and morphine over regular water and drank the drugged water to the point of death. Alexander et al. examined this claim to understand how the rats would behave in socially rich environments instead of in isolation. Alexander et al. provided the rats with a stimulating environment they named Rat Park. Then, they utilized isolated rats as a control and observed how societal and environmental factors could impact substance use.

Their findings would challenge concepts that addiction was a compulsive brain disease. Alexander et al. (1981) reported that rats living in the colony at the time of testing ingested much less morphine solution than rats in isolation. This research suggested that the environment and other possible variables could impact an individual's choice to use narcotics. Sociocultural and environmental variables, in other words, could have played a role in the development of addiction.

While Alexander was doing groundbreaking research in addiction with Rat Park, Lee Robins had produced a similar study, albeit with human subjects, in the decade prior. In her original 1974 research, Robins worked directly with Dr. Jerome Jafee to design a study that would examine soldiers' use of heroin both during active duty in Vietnam and after their return. At that time, President Nixon chose Jaffe to head the Special Action Office on Drug Abuse Prevention and approached Robins about designing the study. Approximately 13,760 army-enlisted men returned to the United States from Vietnam in September 1971. Among these men, about 1,400 produced urine samples that were positive for drugs (narcotics, amphetamines, or barbiturates) at the time of departure. From the population of returnees, researchers collected a simple random sample of 470 men to represent the general sample. From the subpopulation of men with positive urine, they selected a sample of 495 men. This was the drug-positive sample (Robins et al., 1974).

Between 8 and 12 months after their return, the researchers sought out the men for interviews. The interviews covered observations of drug use in Vietnam, opinions as to how the army should cope with drug use, and personal histories in five time periods: before service, in service before Vietnam, in use, family problems, marital history, social relationships, school difficulties, job, arrest, depressive symptoms, psychiatric treatment, and disciplinary action (Robins et al., 1974).

Nearly two decades later, Robins (1993) conducted another study, which included several significant findings. First, the Department of Defense had greatly underestimated the size of the narcotics problem in Vietnam. Almost half (45%) of army-enlisted men in Vietnam between 1970 and 1971 tried narcotics; 34% tried heroin, and 38% used opium. Also, Robins found that addiction was more common than reported. Nearly 20% of Vietnam soldiers said that they had felt *strung out* or addicted to narcotics. Robins and her fellow researchers concluded that the soldiers' claims of addiction were accurate by asking them questions about physiological dependence (i.e., frequency and length of use and withdrawal symptoms). The team also discovered that heavy alcohol use, before and after they entered Vietnam, was almost a prerequisite for narcotic use; in Vietnam, this was inversely correlated.

Although the team gathered numerous quantitative statistics, the core impact of the research was that it challenged the paradigm that anyone who used heroin would most likely become addicted to it throughout their life. Robins (1993) reported that in the first year after their return, only 5% of those who had been addicted in Vietnam were addicted in the United States. Furthermore, even veterans still using narcotics upon their departure from Vietnam were doing well 8–12 months after their return. Robins stated that only 12% of those addicted in Vietnam had been addicted at any time in the three years since their return. Furthermore, for those re-addicted, the addiction was generally very brief. Moreover, Robins reported that it was not the treatment that explained this rate of recovery since only one-third of the men who became addicted in Vietnam received even simple detoxification while in the service and less than 2% of Vietnam-enlisted men went into drug abuse treatment upon their return.

Alexander et al.'s (1981) and Robins's (1993) studies reveal the crucial importance of psychosocial integration on holistic health and wellness and the direct correlation between psychosocial dislocation and increased drug use and abuse. However, while the findings in these studies challenged the previous paradigms of individualized addiction (i.e., the biomedical and psychological origins of addiction study), they also created a new discipline or additional lens for addiction studies to focus on: the sociocultural. Sociocultural variables were now understood as a new origin for addiction. These new variables meant another severing, another prioritization, and another disciplinary field laying claim to the etiology of addiction.

Psychosocial Integration and Disintegration

Rather than treating the sociocultural lens as one factor in the development of addiction, B. Alexander (2008) built a new addiction theory (psychosocial integration/disintegration) through which he claimed could encompass both the root causes of and solutions to addiction. Various theorists have begun to examine and study the link between the sociocultural environment and addiction; however, his hypothesis is conspicuous in that he frames addiction as a culturally created concept. He proposed that the psychosocial disintegration of cultures and communities is one of the key driving factors that produce and perpetuate substance abuse/addiction in individuals. In his work, he traces the historical decay of both early Native American and aboriginal cultures. Moreover, he discusses how this destruction of communities led both cultures to have an enormous struggle with addiction and substance abuse.

In Western medicine's model of addiction as an individual/internal issue, biomedical theorists fail to consider the sociocultural aspects of addiction along with the enormous influence of the environment on human behavior. This limited and narrow view of addiction has kept researchers, academics, and clinicians viewing addiction myopically, as if looking through the eyehole of a fence. Instead, they should rise above the fence to examine and explore addiction holistically and view the multiple layers and continual interplay of variables that drive and perpetuate it.

B. Alexander (2008) discussed how psychosocial integration is key to holistic health because it acknowledges interdependence, provides a sense of identity, provides self-worth, and offers a tangible collective consciousness. However, as much he sought to advocate for a holistic approach to addiction study, he still operates from an interdisciplinary perspective, tracing each arena, yet never examining the relationships between treating addiction as a stagnate entity and not recognizing its multiplistic nature. Furthermore, he drew from the work of Erik Erickson and Karl Polanyi in recognizing the necessity of integrating social belonging and individual autonomy for the achievement of human wholeness. B. Alexander (2008) traced many authors' and thinkers' recognition of the inherent and necessary value of psychosocial integration:

> This central fact of human nature has been recognized by countless other great thinkers as well, notably Plato, Charles Darwin, Peter Kropotkin, Alfred Adler, and Erich Fromm. The importance of this fact is acknowledged by many contemporary social scientists who use a great variety of alternate names for psychosocial integration, such as "belonging," "community," "wholeness," "social cohesion," or simply "culture."
>
> *(pp. 58–59)*

B. Alexander (2008) proposed that without the possibility of adequate psychosocial integration, society creates and breeds a culture of addiction. Hari (2015) advanced this argument in *Chasing the Scream*, linking all addiction processes to a failed attempt at healthy psychosocial connection.

Although Alexander and Hari highlighted the importance of psychosocial integration and the sociocultural aspects of substance abuse and addiction, it is still yet another myopic and simplified theory of addiction as a whole. Once again, they add to the heap of academic theories on addiction, trying to nail it down and give an understanding of why it develops and why it continues to manifest in the lives of individuals, without ever examining how it moves and evolves.

Alexander and Hari claim to have found the true causal roots of addiction and also provide a watered-down and simplified version of the cure for addiction, that of increased social connection. It is important to recognize the value of community connection and to see all the ways that psychosocial integration can help to decrease substance abuse and addiction; however, we must not once again get lost in believing that a "new" theory of addiction has arrived to replace and void all others.

Circling back to the hand of addiction, we now see that Alexander and Hari have taken attention off the other fingers and placed it solely on the middle finger, the sociocultural components of addiction. Minimizing the biomedical (thumb) and psychological (index), they state that all addictions can be healed by simply reshaping society to be more inclusive and connected. We must give credit to Robins, Alexander, and Hari, but we must also begin to acknowledge how they have fallen short and once again stratified addiction study to a molar root and severed the spaces in between by fixating on another finger, the sociocultural.

To fully understand the nuanced impacts that society, culture, and the collective have on individuals, it is important to look at theorists and authors outside of addiction studies. Deleuze and Guattari, Michel Foucault, William Burroughs, and Paul Virilio examined and critiqued the sociocultural in nuanced and unique ways that help us understand the breadth and depth of society. To understand how and why society put years of drug policy into legislation and the war on drugs, it is beneficial to look through the lens of Deleuze (1992) in his writing of *Postscript on the Societies of Control.*

Control Societies

To examine the sociocultural lenses of addiction, it is imperative to look at society as a whole and the various ways it has fed, contributed to, and perpetuated addiction across all social environments. In his work, *Postscript on the Societies of Control*, Deleuze (1992) explored the ever-shifting dominance institutions have over individuals. Machinic assemblages, such as the social, political, bureaucratic, and educational, all impact feedback and produce programs to categorize and control individuals. Deleuze and Guattari (1980/1987) stated,

Understanding the various and complex machinic assemblages that make up and continually produce sociocultural components is key to understanding the holistic and nuanced flow of addiction as a multiplicity. Alexander, Hari, and Robins left out pertinent patterns and relations of sociocultural–political machinic assemblages that Deleuze and Guattari (1980/1987) examined at length:

> One of the fundamental tasks of the State is to striate the space over which it reigns, or to utilize smooth spaces as a means of communication in the service of striated space. It is a vital concern of every State not only to vanquish nomadism but to control migrations and, more generally, to establish a zone of rights over an entire "exterior," over all the flows traversing the ecumenon.
>
> *(p. 385)*

This control of migration has been the state's goal in passing drug laws, launching antidrug campaigns, and attempting to control and regulate the use, flow, and migration of substances throughout various communities and societies. The state has a vested interest in controlling these flows and fluxes of any speed. Drug trade, regulation, the tax system, and drug policy are always tied back to the agendas of the state.

As B. Alexander (2008) argued, society has created continual communal psychosocial disintegration which has ultimately led to a globalization of addiction. However, even more glaring is society's attempt to control and regulate access while simultaneously creating the illusion of freedom.

Deleuze then began to examine what he termed societies of control. Deleuze saw societies of control as the consequence of continual technological growth that deviates from what Foucault (1979) termed "sovereign societies" and "disciplinary societies." Deleuze's work allows for a more comprehensive view of addiction as a multiplicity. If we trace the rhizomatic nature of addiction we begin to see how it has been shaped, modulated, constructed, cut off, rebirthed, strangled, let free, and exploded by systems of thought and control (i.e., legal, psychological, linguistic, educational). We can and will later begin to look at how the entire hand of addiction is merely a result of societies of control attempting to define and segment a flow of intensity. The biomedical, psychological, sociocultural, developmental, and spiritual can all be seen as societal constructions and machinic assemblages/industries trying to control, define, and capture addiction for study and dissection. All the while, we must continue to break society's rigid and stratified mental monocroppings to better observe the flow of intensities that comprise and continually shape and form addiction, which is and has always been moving, growing, expanding, and breathing.

Societies of control produce an environment of enmeshed, 24/7, entangled systems through factors such as exponential technological growth, social media, internet, and the rise of the metaverse. All factors initially create a sense of freedom, but they also create a culture of control. For example, smartphones provide us with constant access to information, media, and knowledge, but they also collect and categorize our data to target and control us.

From schools to professional environments to banks to hospitals, institutions are tracking and turning people into data that can be fed into an autogenerated system that determines our worth. Today, SAT scores, credit scores, school, hospital, and legal records shape our access to college, work, loans, and health care. Individuals have become *dividuals*, and this has contributed to further discrimination against the addict who must now learn to operate in a system with little to no help or hope for rehabilitation.

Deleuze and Guattari's (1972) concept of segmentarity in the ninth plateau of *A Thousand Plateaus, Micropolitics and Segmentarity* is again helpful as a tool for understanding addiction. Reexamining the three lines (the molar/rigid line, the molecular line, and the line of flight), it is clear that the rigid segmentarity of society has defined addiction as a molar binary (i.e., you are either an addict or you are not). Rarely, if ever, does Western culture or society allow individuals to maintain flows of intensity in addiction defining those individuals by addiction alone. Much like the dividual of control societies, the addict is institutionally confined, defined, and mapped. The legal system, police department, schools, and prisons all define and label addiction and drug use and consider the addict a menace to society who should be denied access to education, work, and housing.

To fight against and subvert control societies, we must first develop a new social assemblage community based on mutual liberation, common political purpose, and holistic health and well-being. However, before I discuss my work on formulating this radical new social formation, let me rewind to a reflection of my own experience of drug use, addiction, and the impact of living in a society of control.

Breeding Grounds of Addiction/Becoming Free

From an early age in my teens, I can remember feeling duped, tricked, and bamboozled. As I looked around at the world and the trajectory of growth to adulthood, I was deeply disillusioned. Many people I knew were frustrated with their work, riddled with anxiety, stressed, and overall depressed with life and existence. It was as if they had settled for mediocrity in their day-to-day lives and had lost all sense of vitality, passion, or meaning. The control society was hard at work and, although I didn't have the knowledge to name what was occurring around me, I felt it wash over my soul. I knew deep within my heart that I did not want to fall into this trap to become someone who was bitter with life and sleepwalked through existence. I wanted to feel alive, awake, energized, and passionate. Also, I wanted to find a tribe with whom I connected and could share my passion for life.

At 18 years of age, I connected with two individuals who enormously impacted and influenced my life. I was working at a music store where I met Josh, a Nigerian musician with stretched-out earlobes and an amazingly eclectic taste in all genres of music, and Robert, a Marine reserve with intense energy and kindness that is hard to describe. These two became my brothers and best friends over the next several years. Through them, I was introduced to and began using large amounts of cocaine and methamphetamine. Stimulant drugs are unique in the sense that they offer extreme, unparalleled highs but are coupled with debilitating anxiety, sadness, and depression. My life became an endless quest in search of the perfect high, and before I knew it, I was engulfed in chaos, bleakness, and despair. Whatever speed and intensity of elation and hyper-focus these stimulant drugs would provide, they were simultaneously shutting down other areas of perception and balance in my life.

I initially sought transcendence and speed-of-light flight through my stimulant use. My use was deceiving in that it made me feel alive, alert, and nearly invincible. However, upon coming down, I would face reality and pay dearly for the psychological and emotional high I had experienced. H. Skott-Myhre (2008) described Deleuze and Guattari's lines of flight in the following way:

> Lines of flight, for our purposes here, refer to escape routes from the structuring effects of dominant social forms. They are like a complex array of tunnels under and through society that split off in a multitude of new directions whenever they encounter a limit or obstacle. In this sense, the tunnels have no predetermined direction or endpoint but extend infinitely into the event horizon described above. Such tunnels, or lines of flight, are composed of creative force and provide avenues for movement across and within even the most repressive or oppressive societies.
>
> *(p. 11)*

Drugs had become a false line of flight for me in numerous ways. Substances that once promised avenues and tunnels toward freedom and that increased my creative energy had all but roadblocked my unlimited potential. Deleuze and Guattari (1980/1987) stated, "Instead of holes in the world allowing the world lines themselves to run off, the lines of flight coil and start to swirl into black holes" (p. 285).

The intensity, beauty, and brightness of each high were brilliant and extreme upon entry. Like riding a roller coaster, the climb to the peak filled me with adrenaline, but the ride down from the high left me in a living hell, an unimaginable loss of energy, a death, a destruction of self, and a bleakness and hopelessness that I couldn't put into words. The lines of flight began to coil and swirl into dark, bleak, and black holes of futility around me.

I was no longer the master of my speeds. Whatever benefit or positive results I experienced from drugs intensified and exacerbated the negative consequences of my use tenfold. Deleuze and Guattari's (1987) expression was accurate; my attempted lines of flight through drug use had coiled upon themselves, leading me down and further away from any transcendent high or freedom. For every 20 feet in the air I would soar, I would fall ten times lower, 200 feet below ground. In addition, I was constantly breaking and reconstructing my psychological plane of consistency through energies and flows that competed for voice and stability. Each repeated substance use pulled me further from a true line of flight, promising, but never allowing, a breakthrough or freedom/opening. Rather, each line of substance I ingested initially promised a line toward freedom, yet was always a line to hell.

Ultimately, I began to discover true lines of flight in my life. I discovered areas of pure creative life force within my art, music, family, and life's work of counseling and psychotherapy. I feel profoundly fortunate to have found these lines. In a culture and society where I once felt confined, trapped, and immobilized, I have carved and created lines of flight, tunnels, and traverses to express myself while also working with others to develop and find avenues to fly beyond socially constructed confines. Now that I have located and begun to carve my true lines of flight, I feel the next step of the journey will be creating and constructing societal lines of flight to challenge current culture and its systemically unhealthy and compartmentalized approach to addiction and drug abuse. We must shift how we approach addiction, and it is due time to put an end to the war on drugs.

Through my clinical work with addicts, families, and my collaborative work with psychiatrists, neuropsychologists, counselors, teachers, and social advocates, I educate, introduce, and explain the dangers of the war on drugs while offering unique and creative ways to subvert control societies and find individual truth and holistic growth. Furthermore, I offer and provide new treatment alternatives to addicts and families and speak to various psychiatric hospitals and schools in an attempt to systematically influence organizations and industries to become aware of their barriers. In doing so, I advocate for and direct people toward real lines of flight wherever I go.

In April 2020, I founded and opened an Experiential Therapeutic Community Youth Center called Eternal Strength which provides holistic therapeutic support to youth on the journey of development and growth. Eternal Strength is my line of flight in challenging and systemically changing the language, politics, legality, treatment, and conceptual lens of addiction. Using my own lived experience of addiction, my clinical private practice work with families and clients struggling with addiction, and my now larger youth center, I can clearly see my own journey of growth and my continual fight for a line of flight that allows me to migrate from my own addiction while challenging the psycho and sociopolitical models of control in addiction studies.

We have begun to build a culture, a collective, a mutually liberated sociopolitical, co-collaborative community. If we are going to impact and influence the larger collective, we must form a community committed to fighting against counterproductive antidrug campaigns, abusive and oppressive drug policies, and legislation that oversimplifies definitions of addiction. To challenge the old narrative of addiction and the damage caused socioculturally, we must create new lines of flight to understand addiction as a molecular force and bring about a new sociocultural assemblage of growth and potential.

At Eternal Strength, I have been working diligently to create a community center/mental health holistic treatment center that is an agency of sociopolitical change. Blending elements in H. Skott-Myhre's (2006) paper, "Radical Youth Work," such as humanistic psychology (Rogers, 2015; Watts, 2017), radical systems theory of G. Bateson (1972), postmodern thought of Deleuze and Guattari (1980/1987), nomadic feminism of Rosie Braidotti (2011), and the theoretical work of antipsychiatrist R.D. Laing (1971), I have put into practice a radical approach to working with young people who struggle with their relationship with substances. Our approach is a co-collaborative/mutual liberation community-based program of youth and adults working together toward a common political purpose.

At Eternal Strength, in my clinical work and in my research, I propose that addiction is molecular and migrates and resides in the liminal space between harm and help. Addiction itself is a flux, flow, and movement, a true molecular multiplistic entity with the capacity to turn rigid and molar and stagnate (i.e., abuse and habitual repetition) or also the capacity to break free and create new spaces of potential and growth. More important than giving addiction a concrete definition is the need to continually map and examine the movement of addiction and how it shapes and shifts based on various influences and impacts. How is it that addiction has impacted my life and been so stagnate, molar, and rigid that it leads me to shut down and spiral into a hole of death while at other times addiction has been molecular and allowed me to rhizomatically carve a new line of flight. Addiction is and always will be both, and not either/or.

Before moving further in our discussion of addiction as a multiplicity, we need to tackle and examine the fourth finger in the hand of addiction—the ring finger or the developmental lens of addiction study.

5

DEVELOPMENTAL—THE RING FINGER

DOI: 10.4324/9781003466321-5

Developmental Psychology and Understanding Youth

The dominant discourse of developmental psychology has and continues to evaluate and conceptualize youth (adolescence and young adulthood) as concrete stages in which maturation is sought and ultimately accomplished in adulthood (Erikson, 1950/1993; Hall, 1904; Piaget, 1977; Steinberg, 2001). In addition to adolescence, a new term has arisen in psychology within the last decade called *emerging young adulthood* (Arnett, 2000). Modern psychology defines emerging young adulthood as a time period between the ages of 18 and 25, where an individual experiences identity exploration, instability, impulsivity, heightened self-focus, and a feeling of being in-between (Arnett, 1998, 2000, 2004).

Both adolescence and emerging young adulthood have been associated with and linked to high correlations of substance and drug use (Arnett, 2000; Feinstein et al., 2012). Just as with addiction as a whole, the developmental lens understanding of addiction seems myopic and split (i.e., biomedical, psychological, and social). Developmental explanations of addiction focus on and target adolescent and young adult stages as the breeding ground for first-time substance and drug abuse, which ultimately lead to chronic drug abuse. In particular, they view adolescent development as a time of instability and vulnerability in which substance use and addiction can more easily occur. NIDA stated that teens are more susceptible to substance use disorders due to the malleability of their developing brains. NIDA (2014, para. 3) also noted that the developing prefrontal cortex (arena responsible for assessing situations, making sound decisions, and controlling emotions and impulses) and the parts of the brain dealing with feelings of reward and pain make teens and young adults vulnerable to substance use and abuse.

In modern-day developmental psychology, psychologists conceptualize the adolescent brain as a car with a fully functional gas pedal (reward system) but weak brakes (prefrontal cortex; Dahl, 2004; McKenzie, 2003; Smith et al., 2014; Wallis & Park, 2004). Although this analogy may hold true, it is limited in its ability to fully describe the experiences of young people as a whole and establishes cognitive neuroscience as the origin of addiction. Researchers in this field continually prioritize hormonal growth and brain growth as the primary lens through which to attempt to better understand addictive behaviors in youth:

> Studies investigating key cognitive and neural changes occurring during this maturational period have contributed to the formulation of a "dual systems" model of risk for addiction. . . . Vulnerability to risk-taking during adolescence would therefore be heightened when a fast developing socioemotional system combines with a slow-developing cognitive control system.
>
> *(Castellanos-Ryan et al., 2013, p. 42)*

This calculated and reductionistic conceptualization of youth comes with costs that continually impact and influence the discourse and verbiage we utilize to discuss young people. Much like the biomedical lens of understanding addiction, the biomedical lens of understanding youth development falls short in holistically conceptualizing this period of growth. Seeing youth as merely an amalgamation of biology and neurochemistry lends itself to the dangerous realm of scientific reductionism. Failing to adequately understand the complex, nuanced phenomenological experience of youth contributes to the condescending and often superior stance of "adulthood" explaining young people to themselves.

Instead of viewing a multilayered developmental system at play, such as Ken Wilber's (2000) consciousness developmental arenas or Moira Gatens's (1995) morphological conceptualization of development, youth is categorized as less than incomplete—a brief period that is inadequate or not completely whole. Modes of popular developmental psychology theory (Erikson, 1950/1993; Hall, 1904; Piaget, 1977) contribute to and influence ways of thinking and speaking about youth. Dominant discourse and dialogue are focused on stamping out the youth's voice and pressuring them to conform, adhere to, and perform according to societal norms and functions. K. Skott-Myhre (2016) stated,

> The incorporation of this discourse into the home environment drives a wedge between parents and children that pre-disposes parents to read their children as alien and to treat their behavior as inexplicable. Similarly, as young people begin to experience the efforts by their parents to control and subjugate them, they understandably mount varying degrees of resistance and sabotage. What is lost here is the possibility of a joint understanding of the modes of exploitation and appropriation, by the dominant system of discipline and control that women and children hold in common. Any ability to see common points of struggle, alienation, and marginalization, are obscured by the discourses of development.
>
> *(pp. 181–182)*

If we continue to view youth as a phenomenon to be studied and examined and come to conclusions that we understand youth better than they understand themselves, we will inevitably be met with resistance. Much like the academic study of addiction versus the lived experience of addiction, adolescence must be given voice for us to fully understand the developmental psychology of a human being's adolescent and young adult growth.

How adults view and understand youth has a tremendous impact on the emotions, responses, and communication we have with young people, along with the communication they have with us. If adults see all risk-taking, substance experimentation, and impulsivity as harmful and damaging, they will likely build resentment of youth and create continued disapproval and distaste for growth and exploration. If, however, we begin to understand young people as creative and with unlimited potentiality on a radical pilgrimage (Skott-Myhre, 2016), we may better align with and connect to the depths of the creative life force that exists in all of us. If we choose to listen, youth can breathe life force and creative source energy into our overly rigid modes of task-based "adulthood" existence.

H. Skott-Myhre (2008) challenged the microscopic biomedical understanding of youth and sees youth as "subjectum," or rather the subject that is free to creatively act, to expand better the comprehension of youth/adult relations:

> The subjectum offers child as an attribute that both youth and adults have in common. It suggests that differences in age are non-hierarchical and that differences can be brought together for mutual creative benefit. The alternative subject implied here allows youth and adults to join together in creative collusion against the forces of containment and discipline.
>
> *(p. 9)*

H. Skott-Myhre's (2008) work suggests that we can look at the subject of youth as subjectum, as a radically valuable space of liminality in which creative life force and unlimited potential lives and breathes. Understanding young people as a space of radical openness and potentiality allows us to dive deeper into the realm of lived experience and growth, not merely on the biochemical or neurological level but rather a multitude of growth and awareness arenas: psychological, emotional, social, artistic, relational, existential, and humanistic.

H. Skott-Myhre and K. Skott-Myhre begin to offer pathways to thinking transcontextually to see youth and development as a liminal space of becoming, full of potential and creative life force. Thinking in this manner gives birth to an ecology of mind (G. Bateson, 1972), allowing us to stay open to new paradigms of thought and to continually focus back upon the pattern that connects. Remembering G. Bateson's (1979) search for interrelated connection, we can see all lenses of addiction as intimately connected and continually influencing and impacting each other. Youth can be seen through all the lenses of biology, psychology, sociocultural, environmental, developmental, and spiritual, therefore developmental psychology is never solipsistic, isolated, severed, or apart from; it is always connected, immersed, and interwoven, as is all of human existence.

> If I can begin to see an ecology of my ideas, thoughts, and cognition, then I can begin to see mind in ecology. This is a big shift. The interaction of each organism in its inward and outward relation to its ecology is boggling to hold in sight. The interrelationships of the biological world are

> functioning with an intimacy similar to that of my own thoughts—can I not see the leaves of a plant that turn themselves toward the sun, or the seduction of the colors and perfumes of a flower that lures the bees?
>
> *(N. Bateson, 2016, p. 22)*

The interrelationships are an ecology of mind and a mind of ecology. They are a cross-pollination of ideas and an acceptance of the nature of things not being separate, yet being intertwined and impacting and influencing all that occurs. These relationships of connection are at work everywhere and flow through all of our systems and categorizations, yet we only begin to give them voice when we put our attention to the patterns at play.

The Work/To Be Fully Seen

In my work as a mental health counselor, I have connected with hundreds of young people ranging in age from 10 to 25. I am highly experiential in my work and often find myself engaged in a plethora of activities with clients (e.g., playing guitar, playing pool or ping pong, chess, or drawing and art). Within each space, there are relational connections and entry points to deeper meaning and an understanding of lived experience. As I sit with youth after youth, I am continually fascinated, intrigued, inspired, and also saddened, frustrated, and overwhelmed by them. Each young person has a unique spirit and soul that is walking the radical pilgrimage of youth development (Skott-Myhre, 2016).

Understanding youth development as a radical time of awareness, growth, ego, and identity-seeking and resistance allows us to step away from the reductionist viewpoint of youth just being a developmental phase one needs to accomplish, or as often echoed by adults, "just grow up already!" Young people understand, perceive, and see many of the flaws within society, culture, and the way of being "adults." They struggle with understanding why we must give up play, spontaneity, laughter, creativity, and joy to turn instead to monotony, boredom, and repetitive discipline. Youth are hungry to explore, travel, and experience life at the present moment level. We adults often struggle to be in the present, for the coming future and haunting past continually seduce us to move away from the "now."

The Perfect Storm: Impulsivity, Risk-Taking, and Sensation-Seeking

Impulsivity, a broad term, has been subcategorized in the research literature to examine various factors that make up the whole. Tupes and Christal's (1992) Five Factor Model of Personality presents four distinct facets of impulsivity, including urgency (tendency to act rashly to regulate negative emotions), lack of premeditation (preference for immediate rewards), lack of perseverance (poor concentration on tedious or difficult tasks), and sensation-seeking (penchant for novel situations). Shin et al.'s (2013) work uncovered that lack of premeditation and sensation-seeking are two facets of impulsivity linked most directly to illicit substance use in young adulthood.

Zuckerman et al. (1974) first coined the term *sensation-seeking*, which conceptualizes the degree to which individuals are drawn to risky and challenging activities and behavior. Its correlation to illicit substance use is high (Brill et al., 1971; Huba et al., 1981; Pedersen, 1991).

The impulsivity and sensation-seeking, although correlated directly with substance use and experimentation, are powerful predictors of success in later years in other arenas (i.e., business, entrepreneurship, career development, and social/community justice; Neale et al., 2022). My creativity, becoming-child (Skott-Myhre, 2008), and impulsivity/sensation-seeking are all arenas that allowed me to find true lines of flight in my life, and I am thankful for their existence as without them I believe I would have stayed stuck, stagnate, and frozen in a life of pain and suffering.

Really Live This One Moment

It was nearing evening on a Friday night, and I had brought two of my best friends, Shane and Nathan, into the bathroom of a local Starbucks. We were 17 years old, and I was often pushing boundaries and exploring new and unique ways to get an adrenaline rush. I was doing my best to convince Shane and Nathan that we should strip down naked in the bathroom, hold our clothes and shoes in one hand, leave, and run circles around the outside of the coffee shop. My girlfriend would have the car ready to pick us up and flee. Both Nathan and Shane were nervous and hesitant, so I had to work my magic.

On the one hand, Shane was easy to get on board as all I had to say was "think of how fun it will be, and then how many laughs we will have afterward." Nathan, on the other hand, was dead set against it. He read out a laundry list of adverse outcomes and reasons we should not even think about streaking the coffee shop. Consequently, I had to turn up the persuasion. I looked Nathan directly in his eyes and held up my hand, where each finger represented my words, "Really live this one moment!" After that, Nathan was in, and we all three stripped naked, streaked the coffee shop twice, hopped in the car, and drove away. This was not the first extreme risk we had taken, and it certainly wouldn't be the last. However, I was always the one planning, seeking out, and pursuing risk-taking and sensation-seeking and encouraging the group to join in.

Sensation-seeking had excited my spirit from a young age. I can recall being drawn to experiences that increased my adrenaline and heart rate, whether playing pranks and jokes on my parents and little sister, riding roller coasters, or going on bicycle adventures with my friends around the neighborhood. I was in a continual search of excitement and sensation elevation.

Moving into my late adolescence, my sensation-seeking increased as I began to experiment with substances and gravitated toward peers who were "living on the edge" as well. Looking back upon the underlying current of sensation-seeking embedded in my spirit, I see this energy not as a deficit but rather as a powerful tool. When I was younger, I was unable to fully harness and utilize the energy, and it, therefore, overpowered my reason and led to self-destruction; however, I learned and advanced my ability to channel this sensation-seeking, which has brought immense health and wellness to my growth.

The Dark Side of Sensation-Seeking (Unwielded Energy)

I always craved more: a more intense high, a longer transcendent experience, or a more intense elevated sensation. I can map and trace many experiences of my sensation-seeking, which ultimately manifested in negative ramifications. However, at their core, I felt a yearning to live in the moment and at various levels of consciousness and highs during these experiences. My high school friend, Scott, and I would hop into my Suzuki Samurai 4WD, and the energy was palpable. We both fed off one another and truly felt invincible in each other's presence. I can recall driving down side roads as Scott smirked from the passenger seat with an intense and exuberant grin, asking, "What would you do if I yanked up the emergency brake right now while you were driving?" My reply was often, "I'd roll with it!" We both had electric charges of potentiality running in our veins, and we both knew that this one day was full of surprising possibilities that had no limits. Soon enough, our adventurous energy built, and we took to extreme risk-taking as a way to channel and experience an even greater height of sensation: pumping gas and driving off without paying, shoplifting clothes, driving my mom's 1994 Ford Aerostar van over 100 mph with Scott on the luggage rack screaming, "Faster, faster!" Our days were filled with impulsivity, danger, and cheap thrills. It was mainly our sensation-seeking and lack of premeditation that gave a recipe for the "act first and think later" attitude we brought to everything we did. Scott and I came from different backgrounds. His father was in prison, and he was an only child raised by a single mother trying to make ends meet. My parents were middle class, well-off, and married for over 30 years. Also, I had a little sister and a fantastic support system. However, regardless of differences in our family systems, socioeconomic status, and parental support, we both held the exact same energy, attitude, and spirit of living for the moment, seeking the rush and experience of all that life had to offer.

It is important to mention that this sensation-seeking and risk-taking were done before any of my substance abuse. During the ages of 16 and 17, I had yet to begin experimenting with any substances. Scott and I seemed to seek out these experiences organically. However, at the age of 17, I decided to smoke marijuana for the first time, which was another impulsive and spontaneous decision. Furthermore, I was the one who introduced Scott to marijuana. Ultimately, and at different times, both Scott and I walked away from our use of the drug.

This energy behind impulsivity, sensation-seeking, and risk-taking can be described as radical youth pilgrimage (Skott-Myhre, 2016), youth as creative force (Skott-Myhre, 2008), and becoming-child (Deleuze & Guattari, 1972). Youth as a liminal space of becoming is full of unlimited potentiality. However dangerous and destructive my behaviors, the energy flowing beneath them was always a becoming, a seeking, and an exploratory drive to experience and connect on more profound levels of attunement with self, others, and the ontological nature of existence.

Table 5.1 depicts the relationship between light and shadow, a more profound recognition that each holds elements of the another. The un-wielded

TABLE 5.1 Relationship Between Light and Shadow

Dark/destructive side of sensation-seeking (Unwielded energy)	*Light/growth side of sensation-seeking (Wielded energy)*
I went skydiving four times.	I built a private practice.
I had my nipples pierced at 18 years of age.	I completed a Master of Arts and became licensed.
I had my penis pierced twice.	I work with youth/Vive/experiential work, (skydiving, fishing, biking, rock climbing).
I have too many tattoos to count.	Tattoo journey/reclaimed my body.
I loved roller coasters from a young age.	I work out (i.e., CrossFit, hiking, yoga, meditation, running).
I have been to over 150 concerts.	I got married.
I shoplifted with Scott.	I have children.
I drove Mom's van at over 100 mph with Scott on the roof.	I have my own business.
I stole a bulldozer.	I speak at schools and organizations.
I streaked at Starbucks.	I am living freely.
I set fluorescent lightbulbs outside a door to burst.	I create art.
I hiked while high on crystal meth with no gear.	I am completing my PhD.
I lied, cheated, and stole.	I embody truth, integrity, and ethics.
I hurt.	I am healing.

creative life force gives birth to growth and awareness, which also brings pain and destruction. The wielded energy brings about balance and structure. Moreover, each was needed in my experiential journey of youth growth. I needed to brush up against aspects of myself and go on the radical pilgrimage of my own development. However scary this may be, every young person seeks and will walk this journey in their own unique way. Hopefully, they will learn to harness their individual capacities and channel them with awareness, strength, empathy, compassion, and health.

FIGURE 5.1 The Author at Age 15

Much like the Native American story of the two internal wolves at battle, my journey consisted of a struggle that eventually gave way to me feeding the light instead of the dark.

Becoming-Child

> He remembers love. He remembers water. He remembers solace. He remembers dancing. He remembers being totally free. He remembers no limitations. He remembers energy and creation. He remembers running. He remembers opening the hardshell case of his wine red Les Paul Studio. He remembers Charles Mingus, Jethro Tull, rain, Friday night, the Simpsons, pizza and records forever. He remembers Tina Turner, Simon & Garfunkel, Mahavishnu Orchestra, and playing guitar. He remembers Joe Perry; black, translucent Signature Les Paul, & polishing it until he could see his reflection. He remembers concerts, living in truth, seeing with his ears. He remembers Hana and dancing and skits and freedom.
>
> —Weston Robins

Several years ago, I wrote this text in an Active Imagination class I took during my studies. In the exercise, our class used Johnson's (1986) Jungian Active Imagination technique of free writing. The task involved setting a timer and writing continuously for five minutes without taking a break. In doing so, I attempted to overwhelm my conscious editing neocortex and allow the unconscious mind to emerge in my writing and manifest more clearly. I believed this was accurate and was surprised at the vault of intense internal emotions that I discovered in my five minutes of writing.

All of my memories were from the age of about 12 to 15. The photograph depicts me at 15 years old. That time of my life remains immensely powerful. I believe that I was entering into my first real engagement with the creative life force while also carving and creating many "lines of flight" for the first time. I was experiencing and playing with form, identity, self, ego, and body in many ways. I was artistically constructing myself and my relationship to the world.

At 39 years old, having been married for the last 12 years, and having become a dad to two young daughters, I again feel as though I am embarking on and maneuvering this creative life force energy. Although society defines me as an adult, and modern-day psychology says I am in the middle-aged adult developmental period of growth, I feel more connected to becoming-child than I did throughout my years of turbulent drug use (between the ages of 17 and 24). In the past five years, I have been reconnecting with and manifesting much of my becoming—child energy. In *A Thousand Plateaus*, Deleuze and Guattari (1972) explored what becoming does and does not do in its existence:

> Becoming is a rhizome, not a classificatory or genealogical tree. Becoming is certainly not imitating, or identifying with something; neither is it regressing-progressing; neither is it corresponding, establishing corresponding relations; neither is it producing, producing a filiation or producing through filiation. Becoming is a verb with a consistency all its own; it does not reduce to, or lead back to, "appearing," "being," "equaling," or "producing."
>
> *(p. 239)*

So much of youth development can be seen as a becoming-child. A child, as defined by Deleuze and Guattari (1980/1987), can be seen as an occurrence or event rather than a subject: "The child [does] not become; it is becoming itself that is a child" (p. 277). Rather than viewing development as a linear process in which child becomes adolescent, adolescent becomes young adult, and young adult becomes adult, we can look at the flux and flow of becoming-child as a subjectum of creative life force expression and energy that can be present and occur at any stage at different points in time for subjects.

Deleuze and Guattari (1972) and H. Skott-Myhre (2008) defined a child as an event as opposed to a subject in the traditional sense. Becoming a child as an attribute in all human subjectivity is not simply a stagnant period or developmental stage; rather, it is a creative life force that is active in different ways at different times in the life of a subject. While the dominant forces of sociopolitical and economic organization seek to make child a compartmentalized time period, H. Skott-Myhre (2008) and Deleuze and Guattari (1972) encouraged us to see the potentiality of becoming-child as a flux and flow that runs throughout our lives regardless of age or stages seen in traditional schools of developmental psychology.

H. Skott-Myhre (2008) built upon Deleuze and Guattari's (1987) concept of becoming to examine the creative life force in both youth and adulthood, looking to explore relationships rather than confined areas of structured development. Furthermore, they examined the realm of the subjectum. H. Skott-Myhre (2008) explored how subjectum is defined differently from subject. Subjectum is viewed and seen through the lens of its ability to creatively produce itself. H. Skott-Myhre (2008) pointed to how creative personalities such as artists, musicians, and filmmakers are allowed creative self-production. Children are allowed this space as well, but only from a perspective of developmental growth with constant confinement from adult sovereignty.

The subjectum conceptualization of youth and adulthood would, therefore, seek to understand and see becoming-child as shared by each, a creative life force energy alive and pulsating throughout development and growth as a human being, regardless of age and developmental period.

I believe that in much of my adolescence and young adulthood, substance use was linked to exploration and seeking to understand and explore the creative life force potential. Although I argue that drug use and substance abuse are ultimately a false line of flight, I believe that the initial desire to shift consciousness in adolescence and young adulthood arises from this liminal space of creative youth life force. It is an attempt to explore new terrains and understand and play with self, identity, cognitive narratives, and social constructs. Youth substance use emerges from a desire to experiment and play, ultimately with the realms of the mind and the lenses of perception.

Be Cautious Where You Set Up Camp: Ecological Mind Traversing

In much of my counseling and psychotherapeutic work with youth, adolescents, and young adults, I also work with the parents and family members of my clients. On many occasions, I find myself sitting with families engaged in dialogue and discourse that quickly transforms into parents and adults arguing against substance use (i.e., listing the multitude of dangers caused by alcohol, marijuana, psychedelics, and other illicit substances) while the young client argues for the benefit and even medicinal purposes of various substances. In particular, marijuana is caught in this argument most often. Parents say, "Marijuana is harmful, damaging, and illegal, and therefore, we will not condone or support use in any shape or form." Meanwhile, the young person expresses that "marijuana is medicine, has no negative consequences or impact on health, and actually helps with anxiety reduction and stress relief." I often interject and help move the dialogue to a different, almost meta-level space of conceptualization and exploration.

I share the belief that all chemical compounds can be utilized as either a drug of abuse or a medicine of healing, listing the medicinal uses of various substances, and then quickly demonstrating how each can also be abused and create damaging impacts on an individual's life (White, 2000; Zoja, 2000). I claim that everyone in this world must figure out their relationship with substances. This claim is also useful for many other areas (e.g., food, sex, intimacy, anxiety, and technology). Each individual has a relationship and engagement with these substances and behaviors. Moreover, it is up to us to explore and examine if these relationships are moving them toward health and balance or leading them toward negative codependence and self-destruction. Shifting the exercise to one of exploration first opens up space for clients and families to

TABLE 5.2 Perceptions of Reality

Desert	*City*	*Rainforest*	*Ocean*	*Quicksand*
Marijuana	Alcohol	Sober consciousness	Psychedelics	Other

share honestly as well as space for an in-depth discussion regarding society/culture, psychoeducation, and holistic health.

Using Table 5.2, I sometimes work with families on a thought experiment. I will ask them what ecological terrain they are in as we sit in my office. Many times, all family members are sober and answer, "the rainforest." I then ask them if they would agree that if we all decided to smoke marijuana, we would be shifting our consciousness and headspace to a different realm or perception of reality. They usually agree. I then give them the same example of drinking alcohol, taking LSD, taking cocaine, heroin, or methamphetamine, and comparing each substance to a separate and unique ecological terrain/environment.

All family members usually agree that ingesting various substances would shift them to another realm of consciousness and perception of reality. Then, I sit up in my chair, lean in toward the family, and state the truth, "You are going to get really, really good at and comfortable with wherever you spend the most time!" Every time I use this exercise, the dialogue about drugs being either good or bad begins to shift. Families begin to speak more in-depth about their relationship with substances. We talk about when, why, and how we as humans reach out to substances, what we gain, and what dangers are associated with living in these "other consciousness" realms and not spending adequate time in sober consciousness (the rainforest).

This exercise and analogy emerged from my attempt to break the molar and rigid narratives of substance use and exploration. I had to implement a new way to think about substance use and an individual's relationship with substances. Additionally, the ecological terrains give them a language in which to speak about the territorial traversing of consciousness exploration. More than any psychotherapeutic technique or analogy, clients and families have responded resoundingly well to this. Oftentimes, they will ask for me to provide them with the chart and send it to them again. I have even had clients report how useful it has been in their journey to growth and how they have used this analogy and mapping as a way to move toward health and holistic wellness.

Throughout my work, I continue to see youth with a hunger to explore these various consciousness realms/ecological mind terrains. I sit with them as they share their journeys with me time and time again. Moreover, I try to provide them with reliable and grounded information about substances, tolerance, withdrawal, and the extreme dangers within the realm of quicksand (i.e., cocaine, heroin, and methamphetamine). Much like quicksand, one might jump in, fight, and crawl one's way out; or, like so many, one might jump in and never make it out. Lastly, I encourage and motivate young people to explore the rainforest (sober consciousness) as often and as regularly as possible. I urge them to become familiar with the default setting of their mind, emotions, thoughts, and behaviors while in sober consciousness, learning to understand themselves better and maneuver the stresses and adversity of life. Furthermore, I embolden youth to live in this realm (the rainforest/sober consciousness).

Additionally, I work with youth who travel to the desert (marijuana), the city (alcohol), and the ocean (psychedelics) every now and then but mostly live in the rainforest (sober consciousness). They are often able to remain healthy and balanced while moving toward holistic growth. I also work with several young people who have become stagnated in other realms of consciousness and spend little to no time in the rainforest (sober consciousness). This is where I often see increased depression, anxiety, aspects of psychosis, and a plethora of other behavioral and social negative impacts. Therefore, my continued clinical recommendation for youth is to live in the rainforest (sober consciousness), and if they should choose to travel to other realms, I encourage them to be cautious about where they travel and how long they stay for a visit. Furthermore, I encourage them to learn as much about the terrain in which they wish to journey before they decide to go.

The ecological terrain exercise is but one way I help families free up the rigid language and narratives of addiction. It can provide a pathway to a true transcontextual discourse on addiction. Similarly, we can begin to make significant linguistic and verbal strides in the field of addiction if we implement new ways to talk about addictive energy and addiction in general. The first step is to shift the lens through which we see addiction and allow this new paradigm to steadily break down the archaic and rigid categories that had a stranglehold on our understanding of addiction for so long. If we can change how we think about youth, development, and becoming-child, we can simultaneously change how we think about addiction and the entire field of study and treatment of addiction. N. Bateson (2016) stated the following:

> Conceptual concrete is optional. There are gobs of ideas out there to get stuck on and build castles upon. They are harder to change once they become foundations for other ideas. A lightness in the way we hold

> thoughts gives us room to learn, to shift perspective, and to keep a rigorous humility of confusion.
>
> *(p. 22)*

Thinking with an ecology of mind allows us to utilize conceptual tools which keep ideas flexible and alive in relation to one another and the outside world (N. Bateson, 2016, p. 21). Before delving more into an ecology of mind and its benefits regarding addiction, I tackle and examine the last digit on the hand of addiction: the pinky or the spiritual.

6

SPIRITUAL—THE PINKY FINGER

DOI: 10.4324/9781003466321-6

Addiction and Spirituality: A Brief History

For hundreds of years, psychoactive drug use has been closely tied to spirituality. Studies in the early history of substance use demonstrate that many cultures have used consciousness shifting plants to attune to the spirit realm (Sayin, 2014). Across many pagan and shamanic cultures (African, Native American, Mexican, Nordic, and Greek), people have utilized psychoactive plants in a ritualistic and spiritual manner (Sayin, 2014). In addition, much of the shamanic and healing use of sacred plant medicines has been an attempt to connect, commune, and join with the divine (God, spirit, spirit world, and spirit realm; Crocq, 2007; Zoja, 2000).

As modern-day Western civilization has evolved, many of the sacred rituals and practices have been abandoned and forgotten. Throughout the 1900s, substance use was viewed as damaging, negative, a human moral failing, and a disgrace against God by much of the Christian community. St. Augustine and other early followers of Christianity used religion and spiritual practice as a way to combat worldly pleasures/temptations and fight the pull of addiction on all levels. Seeking a life of piety and asceticism became a way to choose God over the negative and devilish temptations of substances and alcohol (B. Alexander, 2008).

Beginning in the 1930s as AA was becoming a collective organization, spiritual transformation became a key component of the healing and treatment of addiction. Conceptualizing addiction as a biological disease with a spiritual cure was a foundational component of AA (White, 2000). As AA has grown, it continues to gesture to this spiritual foundation of healing, encouraging members to recognize their powerlessness over substances and give their will up to a "higher power" or God, however, they choose to define and identify this (White, 2000). All of AA's philosophy and conceptualizations are mostly based on a transcendent spirituality, seeking to seek and find an external God through a "higher power." AA's spirituality is one of transcendence.

Theological debate, study, and examination are lengthy in history and far too vast and complex to take on for this current project. Still, what is important to name and situate is both the notion of a transcendent God (existing beyond, outside of, or above the range of human experience) and an immanent God (existing or operating within and connected to; Kim, 1987).

Spinoza and Immanence

Spinoza's God is one of immanence. To Spinoza, God is nature, everything that is, an infinite substance that makes everything that exists, has existed, and will exist (Cannon, 2009). To Spinoza, a philosopher of the force of life, life is not a theoretical idea, it is a matter of being itself.

For Spinoza, all substance—immanence, the plane of immanence, God, nature, the material, the infinite, the eternal, the indivisible—is one and cannot be separated. For Deleuze and Guattari (1991/1994, p. 41), the plane of immanence is prephilosophical and not a program, design, end, or means: it is a plane of immanence that constitutes the absolute ground of philosophy, its earth or deterritorialization, the foundation on which it creates its concepts.

Spinoza was a metaphysician, studying and philosophizing on all laws and everything in existence. His main and first principles can be reduced to two statements, "being is one" and "the many is one" (Allison, 1987; Bennett, 1984). What this means is that the many things/everything (the laws of physics, stars, animals, humans, the forest, plants) are all part of one thing: nature. We have a tendency to forget this interconnectedness and view things as separate and independent of one another, hence the separate vies and compartmentalization of the conceptual frameworks of addiction. However, if we reexamine the function, flux, and flow of nature, we begin to recognize the interdependence, interconnectedness of all things. We are made of atoms and require food, oxygen, water, and energy to sustain life. We can begin to see the interdependent ecosystem of life system that sustains all in the plant, animal, and human kingdom. This allows us to see how no true separation or solipsism can exist and still sustain life force energy. Each action affects another and, in short, we recognize that everything is connected (Nadler, 2020).

Spinoza laid out a mathematical, logical, and geometrical pattern informing us that there are three parts to the universe: substance, attributes, and modes (Curley, 1969). Substances refer to what things are made out of while attributes refer to the way we experience these substances, extensions (actual materials), and thoughts (our cognitive interpretations of them). Finally, mode is the form or shape the substance takes. However, Spinoza went on to define a substance as something that is independent in and of itself. By this definition, a leaf or a tree would not constitute a substance then, considering they are dependent on air, soil, and water. This only leaves one substance by Spinoza's definition, which is nature. Spinoza saw Nature and God as one substance and used the terms interchangeably. God, therefore, is not outside of anything and is rather embedded within all things. Spinoza understood that if we studied anything closely enough, we would discover that it was implicated and affected by everything else.

In nature there is nothing contingent; all things have been caused by the necessity of the divine nature to exist and produce an effect in a certain way (Spinoza, 1677/2009). To understand addiction, we must understand ourselves. To understand ourselves, we must understand nature. Moreover, to understand nature, we must understand God, which is all things and the only substance.

Addiction and Spirituality

Spiritual understandings of substance use, abuse, recovery, and addiction are prominent throughout history. Substance abuse has been used to signify a disconnection from a moral God (B. Alexander, 2008). AA recovery has positioned the notion of a higher power as the solution to recovery (White, 2000). Other writers have spoken of the relationship between an attunement to God/the divine or the spirit world and a healing from addiction (Grof, 1993). Finally, others have seen spiritual creativity as a driving force in the nature of addiction (Leonard, 2001).

The field of addiction studies through the lens of the spiritual, however, fails to take into account for the divine within and the plane of immanence as revealing all in existence as God. All living matter and all that is as God/Nature. The majority of spiritual addiction study works with the transcendent God as a tool for healing and recovery (White, 2000) while minimizing or overlooking the healing components of God as pure immanence.

Several experts, authors, philosophers, and researchers (e.g., Zoja, Grof, and Leonard) have attempted to dissect the spiritual lens of addiction, yet have compartmentalized spirituality as separate from biology, society, culture, and development. The question remains: What about the biological, psychological, sociocultural, and developmental lenses? More importantly, what about their connection and relationship to each other? Spiritual studies of addiction largely see these other lenses as nonexistent and spiritual understandings and theories of addiction begin to take over entirely. In particular, AA promised that the cure to addiction is spiritual. Jung's letter to Bill W., Founder of AA (1961), stated that addiction is a spiritual thirst for wholeness and union with God and his formula *spiritus con spiritum*, recognizing union with the Divine as the highest religious experience and relationship with alcohol, and Latin "spiritus" as the most depraving poison. This translates to one experience or the other and seeking to "get high" through addiction as a latent desire to commune with God. Unique and creative understandings tell us more about addiction, yet still represent a severed lens that leaves out the holistic multiplicity that is addiction. Once again, addiction is seen as a stagnate entity with a generalizable cure-all for anyone in the throes of it.

History has done the same with defining God as it has done with defining addiction. A compartmentalization, an encapsulation, a closed-door understanding of a phenomenon that is ever-moving, ever-growing, and ever-flowing in the here and now. We attempt to define God and addiction as if they are definitive. However, addiction exists on the plane of immanence—rather than defining it, we can allow it to move, breathe, and flow and recognize its interdependence. Addiction cannot be separated from us because it is not a substance. Instead, it exists as an attribute of different modes existing in the only substance: Nature/God.

My First Taste of the Divine

The best way I can describe my relationship with the Divine/spirituality/God is to relay a story from my childhood. When I was 3.5 or 4 years old, I was asking my mother many questions regarding God (Is God male or female? What does God think is funny? What kind of job does God have? When can I talk to God? Where is God?) Finally, my mom said, "Wes, take out a sheet of paper and write a letter to God with every question you have." So I did just that. I asked all the questions I yearned to know the answers to. Then my mom said, "Ok, now go bury that letter in the backyard." When I awoke the next morning, she said "well, go dig up your letter." I immediately ran outside to the backyard and dug up the letter and to my amazement it read "Wes, I am neither male nor female, I am in the birds, the trees, the air, and most importantly, your heart. I am inside you and all around you and you can call on me whenever you need!" Though I would eventually learn that my mom had written this amazing response, I still feel this understanding of God and the Divine to be the closest and most descriptive conceptualization I have, and I hold it as truth in my heart.

My mother had set the stage for me early on to begin carving out a sacred space and personal relationship with God. I could now go directly in my own heart and spirit to call on and commune with God whenever I needed. Grof (1993) stated the following:

> Our first-hand relationship with the divine has nothing to do with dogma or politics or personal grandeur. It is not about looking exclusively outside ourselves toward some vague, detached entity that is judgmental and critical. Spirituality has to do with our own private and intimate connection with the limitless and constant essence that dwells within. This is what we yearn for.
>
> *(p. 43)*

Understanding God as all substance began to shift my thinking and allowed me a glimpse of the experience of what Spinoza called immanence (Deleuze, 1970/1988). My mom had gifted me with a way of thinking, but more importantly, with beginning to experience God in all of life. Although she may not have recognized it fully, she was laying out the metaphysics of Spinoza's ethics. **Spinoza (1677/2009)** rejected transcendental phenomena for a plane of absolute immanence.

> Our mind, in so far as it understands, is an external mode of thinking, which is determined by another mode of thinking and this one again by another, and so on to infinity: so that they all constitute at the same time the eternal and infinite intellect of God.
>
> *(p. 222)*

God was with me and was me. I no longer had to ask my mom questions about God, I could directly engage with God and was continually always with God as there was never a separation. My mom had laid out the plane of immanence, and I was now free to explore and move throughout it, knowing that God/Nature was inherent in everything, and all substance was an expression of it, and there was no separation.

Defining God

Philosophers, scholars, and academics have all struggled to define God throughout history (Spinoza, Kant, Hume, Nietzsche, Russell), and many people have aimed to categorize and quantify the realm of the spirit world. In addition, religion and science have long been at odds with one another, which has always intrigued me, as I rarely ever saw them as in opposition to each other. With empirical scientific truth, we seek to measure, weigh, examine, and prove. Meanwhile, with spiritual truths, we focus on the embodied, and ethereal, and often speak in the language of analogy, mythology, and direct, phenomenological experience—two interpretations with two separate goals in mind, yet both seeking to better understand reality. Many religions have also argued that only particular Gods, Goddesses, and deities exist, and to believe in or have a relationship with a multitude of Gods is blasphemy. However, the roots of Christ Consciousness, Buddha Nature, and Krishna Consciousness align well and interplay with one another in a harmonious symphony of peace, love, acceptance, forgiveness, and overall benevolence of spirit (Ram Dass, 1971; Watts, 1973).

Much like G. Bateson (1972), who deconstructed academic subfields (anthropology, psychology, biology, and ecology) as man-made artifacts of categorization, I would argue that religion and spirituality have practiced a similar differentiation and separation of sorts. This sectioning off and construction of separate religions has long caused fear, hate, anger, violence, and destruction all in the supposed name of God. As many try to proselytize and convince others what path of spiritual relationship they should walk, they ultimately fail to recognize that the inner journey of divine awakening is where all the work itself lies:

> These people fail to realize that it is on the inside that God must be defended, not on the outside. They should direct their anger at themselves. For evil in the open is but evil from within that has been let out. The main battlefield for good is not the open ground of the public arena but the small clearing of each heart.
>
> *(Martel, 2001, p. 71)*

As people have and will always debate, argue, and explore the existence of God, it is important to recognize the interconnectedness of all things. The interdependent ecosystem of existence that all are housed and embedded in the plane of immanence or nature/God.

Stones Rule/Music Saved My Soul

I was 12 years old and just finishing up my seventh-grade year of middle school when my dad picked me up from school and told me to open up the glove compartment of his light blue Volkswagen bug. Inside, there was an envelope and as I opened it, two concert tickets fell out for the Rolling Stones, Voodoo Lounge tour. My first live concert was on November 15, 1994 at the Georgia Dome, and it was a spiritual experience. I can vividly remember the goosebumps on my arms as the music blared, and I watched in awe as the Rolling Stones played "Sympathy for the Devil," "Street Fighting Man," and "Miss You." I was simply amazed and I was hooked. I would go on to see over 150 live concerts over the next ten years.

In July 2019, my wife and I were visiting my parents and letting our 6-year-old daughter (Story) and 3-year-old daughter (River) hang with Moose (my dad) and Nana (my mom). I asked my Dad, who was about to turn 69 later that month, to come out to my minivan and open up the glove compartment. When he did, two tickets for the Rollings Stones on July 19, 2019 in Jacksonville, FL fell out. He was amazed, and I considered it a sacred gift to be able to attend this show with him again after 25 years had passed.

Both of my parents have given me the gift of not being afraid to seek spiritual attunement in all of life. My mother allowed me to know that connection with the divine resides within my heart and soul and all of life around me, and my dad gifted me with a love and connection to music that has given me some of the most profound spiritual experiences of my life. I am grateful for them both as I know that without these gifts my life would not be the same.

Once again, my parents allowed me to understand spirituality, divine essence, and God as life. Life is not theoretical, it is a matter of being. A reality not of theory, rationalism, or transcendental idealism but rather of absolute immanence. No dogmas, belief systems, or transcendental truths were forced upon me at a young age, rather I was free to develop my relationship to life and Nature/God in any capacity I saw fit. Much of my parents' unconscious ontologies directly aligned with Deleuze and Guattari's (1972) becoming, Spinoza's (1677/2009) immanence, and G. Bateson's (1979) ecology of mind, and I am eternally grateful for this synchronistic connection. Yet as my use and drug abuse progressed and expanded, something felt disconnected, lost, and misaligned from all that I had ever known. Little did I know that music would, once again, be the healing entity that would save my soul and set me free.

Live at Slane Castle/Perceiving the Plane of Immanence Once Again

I couldn't wait anymore. I knew what I had to do. It was December of 2005, and I was sitting in my loft apartment in Marietta, Georgia. Over the last seven years, my life had been a continual roller coaster of substance abuse and heavy drug use. Although I was not using cocaine and methamphetamine anymore, my marijuana use was anywhere from a half ounce to an ounce every three or four days. I was basically just using to stay high, but at this point, I was no longer achieving any "high," I was simply seeking a numbness of sorts.

I was watching a Red Hot Chili Peppers DVD on my TV, "Live at Slane Castle." As I watched the band play, I began to think about each member: Flea, John Frusciante, and Anthony Kiedis, all dealing with addiction and drug abuse and moving away from destruction and toward health and growth. I began to think of my little sister Hana who was six years younger than me and was highly concerned and worried for my well-being. I had gone from being her big brother and role model to leaving her overwhelmed with fear about my future, whether that be death or prison. Tears streamed down my face as I felt with all my heart the ways I had unintentionally hurt and brought continual strain to my family. I was filled with shame, guilt, fear, anger, and resentment at myself and knew it was now or never that I had to break the molar line of rigidity and move to a molecular space of potentiality if I were to have any hope for a different life.

As I sat in my apartment alone and began to reflect on the past seven years, I became overwhelmed with fear and anxiety, recognizing that my life had been an endless pursuit to achieve the perfect high, and I had continually come up disappointed, exhausted, and empty-handed. I knew in my heart that I would never achieve wholeness or happiness if I continued to have drugs in my life, and my codependent relationship with marijuana was the last tie that I had to cut. It became evident that the last seven years were a continuation of perpetual pleasure chasing, which always ended in deep regret and sorrow. I knew I had to move toward pain to begin to work through it. I could no longer run, for my attempt to alleviate pain only caused more pain.

My life was flashing before my eyes, and I was well aware that I had two clear options: (a) continue to use marijuana and never be at peace nor tune into my true potential in life; or (b) break ties with marijuana and begin to create and carve a life I loved so much that I had no desire to shift consciousness. I am happy to say that that night, in my apartment, December 2005, was my last dance with Mary Jane and my last time living just to get high. Now 39 years old, I am a father, a husband, a son, a brother, a healer, an artist, and a soul, and I can safely say I feel at peace and very certain that the last 17 years of my life have been devoted to growth, awareness, and a redirection of my energy into tuning into my full potential.

Emotional turmoil, three arrests, suicidality, depression, anxiety, loss of friendships, and a tarnished relationship with family—none of these things stopped my abusive and addictive drug use. That night, in 2005, I had a breakthrough, a cathartic awakening, a vision, and a dream of my future. It was as if I was recognizing God/nature/substance/myself, and the plane of immanence for the first time since I was a little boy asking my mom questions about God. I had a choice, I could either continue walking my path of darkness and destruction or turn toward light, growth, awareness, and strength. The plane of immanence and God hadn't changed, rather my use had shifted my perspective lens to one of disconnection, separation, and misalignment. I understood, then, that I would have to reawaken the fundamental metaphysical truth of my being and existence if I wanted to heal. Morgan (1999) wrote:

> In that instant, the individual realizes that not only is the universe not very supportive, it is often cruel and apparently irrational. The individual discovers that to live is to continue to suffer pain. This revelation, although it offers the opportunity for spiritual growth, does so at the expense of possibly shattering the individual's sense of "self." No person's worldview emerges unscathed from this moment of ultimate awareness of one's place in the universe. Upon achieving this ultimate insight, the individual reaches a decision point: She or he may come to reduce his or her "demands to what they can get and do not dream of that which seems to be out of their reach" (Fromm, 1968, p. 21), or the individual might strive to force his or her will upon the universe.
>
> *(p. 39)*

It was time to force my will upon the universe, lean against the heart of God, and wake up to the plane of immanence and nature of reality surrounding me. I was done running from myself and was ready to move toward wholeness.

Immanent Truth

Reflecting back on the earliest formation of my spirituality, I can recognize how this divine light and source of internal truth was something I attempted to recreate in my substance use. The magic of childhood, dreaming, playing, and the unique experiences first offered to me by live music were true "highs." These experiences allowed me to have a truly free and sacred space to explore, play, and move through existence. As I continued to mature in adolescence and young adulthood, I seemed to lose touch with these spaces so that I was perhaps unconsciously trying to break or relieve the banality and habituation of adolescent maturity and responsibility. H. Skott-Myhre (2008) and Deleuze and Guattari (1972) stated that child is a becoming, a place of creative life force, flow, and expression, and the confines of adult sovereignty were more obtrusive the older I got. I still longed to be free to play, and society allowed less and less of this child-like exploration.

H. Skott-Myhre (2008) explained that the adult's "childish" desire to be fully and playfully creative must always be used to benefit the dominant system, and the world of the youth, with its relative creative freedom and capacity for "resistance" and "rebellion," must be created as not only unavailable to the adult but unattractive and unhealthy as well. It was as if I was in a vice machine slowly squeezing creativity and life force energy out of me to expedite my adult maturity and growth, which was solely focused on production and obedience to a consumer, capitalistic society/culture. I couldn't see a future where life force energy was not captured and destroyed, and this in turn created dark despair and intense feelings of nihilistic death.

Much of the process of adolescent development and deeper awareness of life brought about the reality of the inextricable nature of existence and pain. To be alive was to experience the entire spectrum of emotions (i.e., joy, sorrow, pleasure, pain, etc.). However, as growth emerged, the spaces for creative play, exploration, and joy were slowly shut down by societal restrictions and demands, that is, work, school, and various power structures and institutions.

My substance abuse was an attempt to free myself and obtain a spiritual connection, which I felt I had lost. My substance use was a way to fight conformity and attempt to stay in a space of childlike wonder, untouched by the jaded and rigid constraints of society. However, this was a failed attempt, a false line of flight (Deleuze & Guattari, 1972). Rather than breaking free from the assemblage and increasing creative potentialities (line of flight), my substance use slowly but surely turned into a line of destruction.

My substance use was a clinging to becoming-child, a gripping to creative life force play, a scream out loud to not have my voice stifled. I could not see another way to fight the assembly line of death (adult existence) that lay ahead. However, the greatest paradox was that as my substance use may have started as a loud rebellion and defiance of the status quo, it quickly and sadly became an, even more, stagnate line of death and monotony more confined and tortured than the adult existence I feared so intensely.

All of the musicians I admired were still playing, creating, and living each day in a zone of exploratory visions and potentiality. In addition, much of the music that resonated with my soul and spirit spoke of visionary and peak experiences of unitive consciousness, where ego dissolved and another realm of creativity and beauty reawakened. I longed for those moments, where the mundane responsibilities of tasked-based existence evaporated, and people were alive and on fire.

The souls that I found seeking this beauty were always involved with and experimenting with drugs. I had been told at an early age by school, society, parents, and law enforcement to avoid these people and drug use; however, from the ages of 17 through my early twenties, I found that "these people" were the only ones still seeking or so I thought. The friends I met who were using drugs frequently were more spontaneous, more open, ready for adventure at any moment, and could relate and communicate to one another on a deeper level of connection beyond the realm of superficial interpersonal engagements. However, as my use progressed, these open, adventurous, and exploratory free souls became blackened, closed, and rigid. They were habitual, mechanistic, and routine—anything but free and untethered. I and the drug users were calculated, constricted, and premeditated. There was no room for exploration, adventure, or creativity, because the first priority above all else was to obtain and use drugs—not as a way to open creativity but rather as a way to avoid pain and the uncomfortable realm of sober consciousness. Sober consciousness was now boring, stagnant, and dull to the seasoned psychonauts. Our drug use had drained the spirit, beauty, and divinity from the soul. It had made my once organic and effortless relationships with play, creativity, music, becoming, and my internal divine connection nonexistent. I was a walking zombie, craving a mere drop of liquid from the divine wellspring that once overflowed in my heart. According to Deleuze and Guattari (1980/1987):

> Drug users have not chosen the right molecule or the right horse. Drugs are too unwieldy to grasp the imperceptible and becomings-imperceptible; drug users believed that drugs would grant them the plane, when in fact the plane must distill its own drugs, remaining master of speeds and proximities.
>
> *(p. 286)*

In my walk through addiction, I could now see the whole process so clearly. What I yearned for was the plane of immanence, the becoming imperceptible, the line of flight, the creative life force, the nomadic becoming, and playful becoming-child existence (Deleuze & Guattari, 1972). Drugs were alluring and seductive as they presented this offering, but to anyone who has seen the internal throes of addiction, it is quickly recognizable that this promise is a *fugazi*, a fake, a false perception. For the true offering of habitual and repetitive drug use is the complete opposite, the molar, rigid, and stagnate line of black death. Drug abuse kills the creative life force and steals the breath of "becoming" potentiality.

You Never Wore the Necklace, It Was Your Heart and Soul

I used to believe that I had lost connection with the divine, turned away from it, and lost connection with God. Now I recognize I never lost God, and I never could. Spirit, divine, essence, God; whatever name we give the light (god, the divine, immanence, spirit, nature), I carried in my heart and soul. It was never lost nor disconnected and never could be because it was intrinsically linked and connected and not ever separate to begin with. Rather, I had buried it, avoided it, and ignored it. It was always with me, and I believe that divine spark lies and lays dormant in each and every individual walking through the horrors of drug abuse. It is there and always has been with you since you were young. You are not alone, and you can rekindle and build the flame into a bright and beautiful fire of growth, beauty, truth, and unitive connection. Continued substance use will always stifle this flame, like a heavy rainstorm on a firepit of wood. The substances begin to dampen and seep into the sticks, twigs, and kindling, making any spark difficult to light and catch fire. The kindling can still burn; it just needs the warmth and rays of the sun (God, Ra, Immanence, Nature) to dry it and allow it to spark and catch a flame. You don't need to go find God, or to find yourself, you simply need to reengage with the light, fire, and warmth that were within you since birth as an innocent and radiant child of God on the ever-present plane of immanence.

> You don't have to do anything to reach God, to reach enlightenment, to awaken. There is no one who can take you to God. Whoever says they will take you to God is a liar, because you are already there. There's only one living being, and want it or not, resist it or not, effortlessly you are with God already. The only thing left is to enjoy your life, to be alive, to heal your emotional body so you can create your life in such a way that you openly share all the love inside you.
>
> *(Ruiz, 2010, p. 214)*

Whatever hell, trauma, loss, pain, and adversity you have encountered, it is not too late. You can still burn bright with the beauty of the divine soul that lies deep within you. Moving away from substance results in a reconnection, a deeper understanding that you have and hold all that you need within you and your search for and attempt to use substances to find connection is almost like the analogy of taking a trip around the world to find a sacred necklace you think is outside of you and you feel you had lost as a very young child, only to return home and find it isn't a necklace at all, rather it is your beating heart and spirit essence, peacefully embedded and interlinked with your soul, waiting for you all along. "Vocatus atque non vocatus, Deus aderit."

> You were searching for God, and you found God within you. God is no longer there, outside you. When you know that the power that is Life is inside you, you accept your own Divinity, and yet you are humble, because you see the same Divinity in everyone else. You see how easy it is to understand God, because everything is a manifestation of God. The body is going to die, the mind is going to dissolve, but not you. You are immortal; you exist for billions of years in different manifestations, because you are Life, and Life cannot die. You are in the trees, the butterflies, the fish, the air, the moon, the sun. Wherever you go, you are there, waiting for yourself.
>
> *(Ruiz, 2010, p. 214)*

There I was again and always had been, a young soul, an older soul, a becoming-child on the plane of immanence seeing truth, beauty, life, and essence, alive and awake in the hands of God/nature/life, and all substance that is. I had traveled around the world looking, seeking, and searching for a God outside myself, a transcendent essence. Rather, just as my mother had told me in her letter at the age of four: God was everything and everything was God, life force energy, essence, and all being here and now and forever more. Throughout my life, I had sought to stand in the heart of God and nature, but I was already there and had always been, ever connected, inseparable, and whole.

Although the spiritual lens deeply impacted multiple facets of my life, it was still an arena mostly seen as separate from or above or beyond all others. Rarely was the spiritual embedded within, immersed in the immanent. Now that I have properly explored each finger on the hand of addiction, I will review and reveal how addiction is none of these and all of these facets simultaneously.

7

PLAYING JAZZ

DOI: 10.4324/9781003466321-7

My project is to use this writing as a map of addiction. I have compiled and traced the long separated and segmented fields of addiction study to ultimately reveal how they capture and hide the true nature of addiction. I have examined theorists in the biomedical (thumb), psychological (index finger), sociocultural (middle finger), developmental (ring finger), and spiritual (pinky) fields, who each lay claim to the etiological, epistemological, and ontological meanings of addiction. This map is a performance, a becoming, a removal of blockages in BwOs, and an attempt to fully open BwOs onto the plane of consistency (Deleuze & Guattari, 1972). Here, I map an ecology of self, mind, society, and culture to reveal and give voice to the patterns that connect them (Bateson, 1979).

Deleuze and Guattari (1972) defined BwOs as the unregulated potential of a body without organizational structures imposed on its constituent parts, operating freely. Bodies, in this work, refer not simply to physical bodies but any body of composition (theoretical, virtual, philosophical). The BwO is a machine, a form of experimentation that frees the human animal from its instinctual determinism. The BwO cannot fully be reached but rather is always being attained and sought after. However, pursuit or movement toward the BwO can easily become botched and faulty (via the drugged body, the masochist body, the schizo body, the paranoid body, and the hypochondriac body; Deleuze & Guattari, 1972).

The BwO is constantly moving between the surfaces that stratify it and the plane that sets it free. However, the attempt to become a BwO is itself a becoming, a seeking, and an experimentation with possibility. Becoming is a process through which I move toward a revelation of the plane of immanence or the plane of consistency. Understanding addiction as an assemblage and mapping its modes and forms allows us to see its true potentiality. In this project, I aimed to stimulate thought and to promote continued research to better understand addiction as a multiplicity of assemblage of movement rather than a definitive substance. Let us now eradicate this molar/rigid and archaic view of addiction, which has plagued the fields of addiction study for far too long.

The writings and chapters I composed offer readers an invitation to think differently about addiction and to begin to see the organic nature and flux of addiction as continually forming, shaping, deconstructing/deterritorializing, and reshaping/reterritorializing again. In the language of Deleuze and Guattari (1980/1987):

> Every rhizome contains lines of segmentarity according to which it is stratified, territorialized, organized, signified, attributed, etc., as well as lines of deterritorialization down which it constantly flees. There is a rupture in the

> rhizome whenever segmentarity lines explode into a line of flight, but the line of flight is part of the rhizome.
>
> *(p. 9)*

A rhizome has four distinct principles:

> (1 and 2): any point of the rhizome can be connected to any other, it is non-hierarchical, 3: rhizomes have the principle of multiplicity, 4: rhizomes have the principle of a signifying rupture (if a single point of the rhizome is destroyed, it will start up again on an old line or a new line).
>
> *(Deleuze & Guattari, 1980/1987, pp. 6–7)*

Addiction is a rhizome, a multiplicity, that can never be destroyed but merely replicates and springs forth at a different intensity and in a new flow. Drug abuse and behavioral addictions may fold in on themselves and maintain habit, repetition, and rigidity at their core, but addiction itself can either become rigid and habitual or break free and birth a new line of becoming.

In addition, Deleuze and Guattari (1980/1987) examined territories; the environment of a group or the environment of a single person (his or her social environment, personal living space, or his or her habits) can be seen as a "territory," in the psychological sense, from which the person acts or to which the person returns (Günzel, 1998). Processes of deterritorialization and reterritorialization occur in territories.

> Processes of deterritorialization are differentiated again by GUATTARI into "relative" and "absolute" deterritorializations: whereas relative deterritorializations retain the possibility of reterritorialization, absolute deterritorializations are marked by the impossibility of being territorialized again. In that sense reterritorializations are always absolute and never relative, as they per se lead back to a territory.
>
> *(Günzel, 1998, p. 140)*

Relative deterritorializations are transcendent as the territory functions as a transcendent reference, like reterritorializations. Only absolute deterritorializations, however, produce immanence—the transcendent meaning outside of and the immanent within. Addiction has the capacity to operate as both modes and functions. Addiction can function as a relative deterritorialization/reterritorialization leading it back to the territory of a drugged body, yet it can also offer the potentiality of an absolute deterritorialization, a line of flight, and a becoming of a BwO on the plane of immanence.

Deleuze and Guattari's verbiage and tool kit of concepts allow a new opening through which to understand addiction. Rather than conceptualizing addiction as a concept, a substance, or an entity, I would argue again that addiction functions as a rhizome, a multiplicity, and an assemblage. It operates in the space of the molecular and in between, having the capacity to shut down on itself (substance abuse/drug abuse) and also the potentiality of creating new modes of being (art/creativity).

Addiction has moved and continues to flow as a rhizome. However, the fields of study continue examining addiction as if it is a root structure, defining it in stagnate and confining terms, treating it as an independent and separate substance. Those in the biomedical field look at the influence of biochemistry on addiction, psychologists focus primarily on the addict as subject, sociocultural theorists primarily understand addiction as a societal phenomenon, developmental theorists characterize youth and adult growth phases as the main causes of addiction, and finally spiritual theorists view addiction as a consequence of a spiritual deficit.

I utilized Deleuze and Guattari's concepts as tools to expand thought (double bass), Gregory Bateson's tools of patterns, systems, and relationships (drums and percussion) and my autoethnographic experience (piano). The writings in the previous five chapters have allowed me to warm up, practice, jam, and find a rhythm; now it is time to play. Overall, it is the combination of Deleuze and Guattari's thought tool kit, Gregory and Nora Bateson's new epistemology, and my autoethnography that led me to this conclusion. I am hopeful this project will birth others—both my own and others.

I propose addiction is a multiplicity that grows rhizomatically, that can reterritorialize and become rigid and segmented, or that can break free and become a deterritorialized line of flight. Substance use itself holds these same elements. No drug or substance is inherently evil, rather it is an individual's relationship and use of the substance which leads them to molar rigidity (stagnation, habituation, repetition) or to potential lines of flight (creativity, spontaneity, play, expression). G. Bateson (1979) made the following statement:

> You have probably been taught that you have five fingers. That is, on the whole, incorrect. It is the way language subdivides things into things. Probably the biological truth is that in the growth of this thing—in your embryology, which you scarcely remember—what was important was not five, but *four* relations between pairs of fingers.
>
> *(p. 56)*

Addiction is a hand, and the field of addiction studies has created and mono-cropped addiction, to use Nora Bateson's phrase, into five clear and distinct separate categories (i.e., biomedical, psychological, sociocultural, developmental, and spiritual). This mental monocropping is "dangerous, quite literally fucking with the soil of ideas and who we can be as human beings, where we can show up" (Bateson, 2016). Instead, we must continue to fight for what G. Bateson (1979) described as a metalogue or a conversation about addiction where the dialogue is such that the participants discuss not only a given problem but also the structure of the conversation as a whole. We must examine the spaces in between and the interconnected nature of each finger; if we look closely enough, we will see that these categories are one and the same, and all exist on the plane of immanence/all substance/nature.

The Pattern That Connects

Our body/mind is a rich ecosystem of interconnected organs that impact and influence each other. None of them can be separated from one another because "[i]f expertise is specialized, then strangled, profiled ideas become the currency, and I am broke and we are broken" (Bateson, 2016, p. 19). The pattern that connects these ideas runs deep, and it is not a question to be answered but a continual thread to be explored and expounded upon as we learn the interwoven tapestry of life. "Just keep going; don't stop. Keep pulling the thread and mental process and biological structure will come to mirror one another" (Bateson, 2016, p. 22).

It would be a highly simplistic conclusion to say that addiction is a totality of all the previously mentioned fields and disciplines of study (i.e., bio, psycho, social, developmental, and spiritual). Many can see some truth in this; however, much like her quote, we must look further. It is not that addiction has five fingers; this is incorrect. It is our study and disciplinary academic categories which subdivided and constructed these fingers "[b]reak the pattern which connects and you necessarily destroy all quality" (Bateson, 1979, p. 8).

If we map the relationships between each, we begin to watch the walls or false separations slowly dissolve. The mental monocropping and independent disciplines borders begin to be revealed for what they truly are, fabricated confines that have compartmentalized and oversimplified particular modes and forms. My genetic biological composition is in constant interrelationship with my thoughts and emotions (psychology), which in turn is in relationship with my surrounding environment and sociocultural influence. How I think, how I feel (psychology) immersed in a sea of relationality to my biochemistry and my sociocultural surroundings. My biology, my psychology, and my sociocultural environment, all influenced, impacted, and affected by my age and developmental growth. How my culture sees my age and development, what it allows and doesn't allow, impacting and effecting all psychology, meanwhile all these psychological and biological systems are also being influenced by hormonal growth, brain development (biological) and thought formation, self-narrative, ego/identity development (psychology) in an inseparable interlinked web. Lastly, all these arenas are being infiltrated and impacted by my belief system regarding spirituality and the larger functions of the relationship between belief and the spirit realm (i.e., epigenetics and biology of belief; Chopra, 2015; Lipton, 2016).

Everything is connected and swirling in a web of relationality, a never-ending soup of cause and effect. When examined closely enough, we begin to see how biology (the thumb) is impacted and influenced continually by all the other conceptual lenses (the fingers). Looking into biology, we see how it impacts our psychology, sociocultural, developmental, and spiritual lenses. We can do this for each arena, and we begin to understand the web of interconnected relationality, with an infinite set of patterns and connections.

Addiction is all and none. Addiction is rhizomatic, a multiplicity, there is no hierarchy of points or positions such as those found in a structure, tree, or root; there are only lines. Addiction ceaselessly draws connections between semiotic chains, organizations of power, and circumstances relative to the arts, sciences, and social struggles. Deleuze and Guattari (1980/1987) stated,

> To be rhizomorphous is to produce stems and filaments that seem to be roots, or better yet connect with them by penetrating the trunk, but put them to strange new uses. We're tired of trees. We should stop believing in trees, roots, and radicles. They've made us suffer too much. All of arborescent culture is founded on them, from biology to linguistics. Nothing is beautiful or loving or political aside from underground stems and aerial roots, adventitious growths and rhizomes.
>
> *(p. 15)*

Rather than attempt to lay claim to a new theory of completeness or an ideal model of addiction, this project is an attempt to break free from these repeated errors of epistemology. At all costs, we must fight the continual capture of addiction by fields trying to define, organize, structure, and create a set of laws as to what ultimately is a rhizomatic energetic field of becoming.

I am a holistic human being. My being can be seen through biological, psychological, sociocultural, developmental, and spiritual lenses. I was raised in the United States, but my ancestors came from Europe, Scotland, and Italy. The biomedical model of addiction tells me I have a brain disease and broken brain chemistry and abnormal dopamine and serotonin receptors and a hyperactive neurological reward system.

The psychological model of addiction tells me that I have taken substances to cope with internal pain and trauma related to my lived experience. The psychological model of addiction goes on to tell me that I have struggled to balance appropriately my ego, Id, and superego and also that I need to create a new cognitive narrative of identity, ego, and persona to heal and recover from my addiction.

The sociocultural model of addiction tells me that psychosocial disintegration has created the individualistic and capitalistic society I live in and that this environment has manifested my past substance abuse. The sociocultural model of addiction also tells me that my individual biochemistry and psychology are not the cause of my addiction; rather, it is my environment and society at large that have exacerbated my tendencies to lean toward addiction to begin with.

The developmental model of addiction tells me my drug use was simply a phase, an underdeveloped prefrontal cortex, a childish exploration, an adolescent rebellion driven by a burst of impulsivity and risk-taking in a phase called youth and emerging young adulthood.

The spiritual models of addiction tell me that my drug use was an attempt to fill a spiritual void, a craving for a transcendent experience, a yearning for God and community with the spirit realm outside of myself. The spiritual model also sells me the guarantee that only through alignment with the divine and spiritual connection with a higher power will I ever heal from addiction and remain sober.

The theories of addiction all view addiction as a deficit, seeing only its damaging aspects and destructive components. Rarely if ever does any theory view addiction as redemptive, empowering, purposeful, and filled with creative potentiality.

Bateson's emphasis on patterns, relationships, and systems and Deleuze and Guattari's work on rhizomes, becoming, and lines of flight are truly the only theoretical tool kits that have allowed me to capture my holistic experience of addiction. Ever-present, ever-connected, and interwoven throughout all of life, addiction is life force potential. My addiction is an energy, current, drive, tool, forcefield, and gift. It is an integral part of my being and therefore resonates and flows throughout all facets of who I am as an entity. To try and chop up my addiction into one lens of understanding is to simplify a complex mode of subjection.

I am addiction and I am not addiction, all at once. Addiction defines me and also deconstructs my being. Addiction is a malleable tool that at any point can either destroy or bring life to my journey of development. It is this energetic current of addiction that runs deep in my bones. I have held it with me always. It has simply manifested in my life in different modes and forms. Addiction is neither inherently good nor evil; instead, it depends on how an individual utilizes it and stands in relation to it. Much like a sword, one can plunge the blade against one's own skin and self-destruct, or one can wield the blade as a tool of growth, liberation, and empowerment. I have chosen the latter.

My journey of addiction has been a beautiful tale through which I learned my own power and wielded my unique energy to create freedom, clarity, and growth in my life. Rather than allowing addiction to bring rigidity, imprisonment, and destruction to my life (the molar line), I have taken its essence and channeled it to a current of lifeforce and beauty (a line of flight) as I move through existence. My practice, my wife, my daughters, my family, my friends, and my clients have all come in abundance when I am channeling and redirecting my life force of addictive energy toward health. In my earlier years, I allowed this overwhelming energy to take hold and steer. It was too powerful, and it soon overthrew me and dug me into fixation, rigidity, and habituation.

In the last 17 years, I have wielded and channeled my addiction to give birth to beauty, creation, and lines of flight I never imagined possible. As I sit to write the final paragraphs of this dissertation, my wife Alison is putting our two daughters, Story and River, to sleep so they will be well-rested for school tomorrow. I am overwhelmed with emotions and reflect on my journey of growth. Without my addiction, I would not be the man I am today and do not believe I could have achieved all I have.

Over the last two years, I have segued my private practice and opened up an Experiential Therapeutic Youth Center called Eternal Strength. We have an amazing team of therapists, coaches, mentors, and healers who have provided holistic mental health support to hundreds of families and youth. The last two years have been filled with excitement, exhaustion, stress, fear, faith, growth, and beauty. And it is my addiction and the nature of this energy that have allowed me to keep pushing and bring all my dreams to fruition. I have fought to stay driven, focused, and engaged on one goal, and that is the creation of a center that will help youth on the journey of growth. My heart is full of pride and gratitude for all those who have chosen to walk this journey with me. And I know and believe it is my addiction and holistic being that has allowed me to create and bring this vision to life.

Addiction can be beautiful and tragic, joyous, haunting, life-giving, and life-destroying—it is molecular. Addiction is an assemblage in flux, not a stagnate entity. If you are to utilize addiction for positive growth, what matters most is your understanding of the pattern that connects and your constant fight to create lines of flight and not become molar, rigid, or stuck. To attempt to strive to be a BwO. Deleuze and Guattari (1972) wrote, "Find your body without organs. Find out how to make it. It's a question of life and death, youth and old age, sadness, and joy. It is where everything is played out" (p. 151). Addiction is a rhizomatic, multiplistic energy, so be careful where you channel and direct it for it grows quickly and is oftentimes unstoppable with momentum in any one direction. However, if you can seek a line of flight, strive to be a BwO (Deleuze & Guattari, 1972), uncover the interconnected web of relationality, and move toward an ecology of mind (Bateson, 1972), then there is a chance that addiction can prove to be a becoming of an unlimited creative life force for expression (Skott-Myhre, 2008) through which you seek goodness and perfection (Deleuze, 1970/1988).

Inspired by the conceptual frameworks and poetry of N. Bateson (2016), I utilize her template to highlight my own "Identity with an I": "I can imagine that I am just the person in my head and the skin bag I live in, pretending that I am not":

- My mother and my father
- My children and my friends
- My wife
- The families I work with
- My clients, friends, and community
- The food I have eaten and the thoughts that I have
- The heat of the sun and the mold in the earth
- The streaming water
- I am the embers in the fire
- A microbiome of ten trillion creatures
- The land, ideas, and names of my nation
- The current embodiment of 200,000 years of Homo sapiens moving around the globe
- An artist, a musician, a writer, a father, a husband, a brother, a son, a friend, a therapist, a leader, a soul
- 70% water
- The rest is mostly muscle and tissue, bones, and squishy stuff
- I am complex
- I am a dream
- I am an ecology of selves
- Before all else, we are of the ecosystems

Before all else, we are of the ecosystems. I can easily finish the phrase "I am" with air, water, cells, atoms, organs, bacteria, a rich interdependent ecosystem, and web of relationality connecting me to everything in existence. Follow the lines, and they always lead to the larger relationships and connectivity. I am connected, I am part of it all, I am not separate, I am/we are One.

So how then might we use addiction, understand its movement, map its flow, and tune into its capacity to affect and be affected? We must continue to utilize the tool kit and frameworks of Deleuze and Guattari, Gregory and Nora Bateson, and our own experience with the flows and intensities of addiction. Next, we must heed the words of Deleuze and Guattari (1972), informing us on how it can be done:

> Lodge yourself on a stratum, experiment with the opportunities it offers, find an advantageous place on it, find potential movements of deterritorialization, possible lines of flight, experience them, produce flow conjunctions here and there, try out continuums of intensities segment by segment, have a small plot of new land at all times. It is through a meticulous relation with the strata that one succeeds in freeing lines of flight, causing

> conjugated flows to pass and escape and bringing forth continuous intensities for a BwO.
>
> *(p. 161)*

Live your life on a stratum (sociopolitical institutions of capture), develop a deep understanding of our common power as members of the same society, and find a place on the stratum that serves as a line of flight. My addiction began to shift when I lodged myself on a stratum, utilizing the energy I gave to addiction to self-growth, the pursuit of a degree, licensure, and a title that gives me the potential to exert influence upon and in the world of institutions.

Constructing and birthing Eternal Strength, refining and utilizing radical youth work, giving voice to my journey of addiction, and helping others find their voice, and see a way out through a creative and expressive process of becoming, becoming minor, becoming imperceptible, becoming nomadic is my mission. I wanted to defy and resist the institutional definitions of addiction that attempted to contain and define my nature as an addict in need of recovery. I had to find my own voice and fight for the capacity of my addictions to provide a rebirth and line of flight out of stagnation. Finally, through this meticulous engagement with the strata (the biomedical field, the field of psychology, the arena of the sociocultural, the field of developmental studies, and the field of the spiritual), I have sought to create fissures and cracks that can create lines of flight that bring forth intensities and possibilities for BwOs. In doing so, I seek to understand the patterns/connections and interdependent ecosystem of relationality embedded in all nature.

My addiction has become a platform, a springboard, a rhizomatic intensity and flow that allows for growth and a flight toward goodness and perfection. However, it is only when I lodge myself on the stratum and continually experiment with potentialities that I can harness the power of addiction for good.

I no longer view the word addiction in the same manner as society has chosen to define and compartmentalize it. I see addiction as energy, potentiality, and unlimited creative life force—a powerful flux of intensity rhizomatically growing on the plane of immanence. In this sense then, I am an addict—an addict for love, an addict for truth, an addict for self-expression, an addict for experimentation, an addict for becoming, an addict for growth and beauty and strength. Most simply stated, I was once an addict lost, but now, I am an addict found.

8

WORKING WITH ADDICTION

DOI: 10.4324/9781003466321-8

Intro

Methodologies, institutions, organizations, belief systems, alongside a multitude of approaches to working with addiction each claim to harness the holy grail of the perfect approach to help those suffering with addiction. Rampant debates between abstinence-based recovery and harm reduction/risk reduction flood the field of addiction treatment. Once again, methods to treating addiction are strangleheld by a tension between biological, psychological, sociocultural, developmental, and spiritual epistemological and ontological underpinnings. Even the holistic mind/body/soul and biopsychosocial addiction treatment programs oftentimes operate from a place of authority in understanding what addiction is and the necessary steps which should be taken to heal or cure the individual "addict."

My goal for this chapter is to reveal an anti-methodology or true deterritorialized approach to working with addiction. Not a programmatic system with steps, which individuals follow, rather a unique approach to listening to, dancing with, and joining alongside the rhizomatic flow of addiction as it manifests in each individual soul-seeking solace, relief, growth, or freedom.

In my private practice as well as my mental health community center, Eternal Strength, we work with addiction from all angles. We allow it, dance with it, listen to it, and ultimately learn from it through our clients, families, and community. We are oftentimes asked, are you an abstinence-based program?; do you encourage clients to take drug screens?; are you faith based?; do you utilize the 12 steps? The answer to all these questions are, yes and no. Everything depends upon the family and client being served and what they are seeking in their journey of growth/recovery. Before we ever begin work with a client or family, we sit with them and truly try to understand the unique woven tapestry that is their transcontextual being. Making sure to avoid myopic symptomatology and over pathologization, we seek to understand the rich complexity that comprises this unique human soul.

Addiction Treatment Field

Much of the addiction treatment field has become more focused on monetary gain and big business growth and development at the sacrifice of ethical integrity and true client care. Programs promising they have the cure for addiction and profiting off of desperate families seeking help for themselves and their loved ones. First, it must be stated that there is no cure for addiction, because addiction is not a disease. This is a highly controversial statement, but perhaps a bit of semantic unpacking with help provides clarity. Addiction, as I have stated previously, is an energy, a flux and flow of rhizomatic growth. Addiction is unlimited multiplistic potentiality ranging on a spectrum from molar rigidity to molecular becoming and true deterritorialized lines of flight. For us to call addiction a disease is to compartmentalize addiction from a medical lens as an ailment or deficiency often linked to the Westernized biomedical understanding of addiction.

For us to call addiction a disease from a social lens is to acknowledge it as a particular quality or habit adversely affecting a large group of people. Although these statements could be argued to be true, they remain lacking in revealing the whole picture. What about the beautiful and amazing art, music, community organizations, businesses, and socially beneficial creations that are birthed from the realm of addiction? Couldn't we argue that for all of the horrors, suffering, and pain lived by individuals dealing with addiction, there is simultaneously the same amount of beauty, growth, healing, and abundance springing forth from the very same energetic flow and flux?

Too often, we like to label individuals struggling with addiction as broken, damaged, and diseased. This belief system can oftentimes result in a perpetual cycle of guilt, shame, and apathy leaving the individual feeling utterly exhausted and stripped of hope for any potential future of joy or peace. This is why it is absolutely necessary we begin to look at addiction from a transcontextual and individual case-by-case position.

If we continue to take such a complex arena of study as addiction and strip it of its complexity to overly generalize shared aspects, we will ultimately loose the soul of what is occurring for the person. It is crucial we understand the complex patterns that exist unique for all different individuals: What intricacies and differences lie between the 15-year-old girl who self-harms daily and abuses fentanyl, to the 47-year-old neurosurgeon who drinks a handle of vodka a day and consumes several grams of cocaine throughout the week, to the habitual gambler who has lost his life savings at casinos, to the ultramarathon runner who has won countless awards for obsession and fixation in this sport, to the talented and wildly famous guitarist who has devoted his life to music and still plays guitar for a minimum of eight hours a day. Each person exhibiting addiction, but for different reasons, different energies flowing, different internal lives being lived, different people all together, each richly complex and nuanced. Following the rhizomatic flow of addiction we begin to see complexity taking shape in different ways, some destructive and some creative, all addiction.

If we look at only the damaging and deficit portions of addiction, we will ultimately look for the deficits of that human soul. Therefore, I propose that no matter the methodological approach to working with addiction, we see the beauty and potentiality in a human soul to turn from the molar rigidity and stagnation to the becoming and seeking of a BwO line of flight on the plane of immanence.

In practice, this involves a true transcontextual approach to working with others. Not simply a watered-down holistic biopsychosocial assessment of an individual but rather a true understanding of that person's nature and subtleties, alongside their inter and intrapersonal relations to family, education, art, culture, food, body, spirit, technology, ecology, and existence as a whole. If we take away the contextual richness of the human soul, we merely become automaton machines assessing a superficial level understanding of addiction and also of human emotion, behavior, and existence.

Everyone Is an Addict

Many healers, therapists, psychologists, and psychiatrists operate from a standpoint of themselves being "non-addicts" helping their "addict" clients. However, if we dive in more directly, we uncover that each one of us harnesses, wrestles, and dances with the energetic forces of addiction. The licensed counselor who sits with alcohol and illicit drug abuse clients session after session, only to go home and compulsively check social media for hours on end while habitually consuming food she has told herself she doesn't want to eat anymore, yet finds herself impulsively pulled to do so day after day. The psychiatrist who reluctantly prescribes countless amounts of benzodiazepines to clients suffering from anxiety, worrying about the tolerance and withdrawal symptoms being created for his clients, who himself goes to the gym twice a day, no longer as a means to balance health but as a relentless pursuit to achieve the Hollywood aesthetic six pack he longs to have in the fitness magazines he reads daily. The spiritual/energetic healer who utilizes sound healing and chakra cleansing on her addicted clients, who has gone into debt herself from purchasing stones, oils, and crystal sound bowls with credit cards she doesn't have the money to pay off, yet continues to do so habitually even at the expense of her children needing new clothes.

The drug abuser, the shopaholic, the gambler, the fitness addict, all people, all complex, all addicts, some seen by society as acceptable and normal, others outcasted as diseased and broken and some seen as delinquent and immoral. Each life a rich complexity of relational energies begging to be seen, understood, and explored rather than assessed, defined, and treated by a homogenous mental health industry profiting on the backs of suffering individuals and their families.

Understanding the Human First and Addiction Second

Why are you the way you are? Was it your upbringing, your psychology, your family system, your culture, your experiences? To explore these questions at the level of true understanding, it would be crucial to sit with the person answering and delve into a true understanding of how they think and behave.

Much like the left hand side of Ken Wilber's Integral Quadrants from his Integral Theory (1997), the focus would be primarily on the internal aspects of the individual and the society they live in. The individual, idiosyncratic, and intrapersonal exploration is absolutely crucial when working with addiction.

Rather than approaching the addiction head on, we must understand this human soul and where they are in their journey of growth and development. Then a co-collaborative unpacking process would be necessary to begin to connect, build trust, and hold a sacred space for this person to reveal aspects of themselves they have been afraid to look at or accept with themselves and others. Through this process a great deal of healing can occur in which someone begins to feel that whatever guilt and shame they hold, they are not alone in their suffering.

Many therapeutic practitioners overly complicate the knowledge, skillset, or training they feel is needed to work with individuals maneuvering addiction. Oftentimes, just listening and carving space can be deeply healing for anyone traversing addiction. Becoming more genuinely curious about the person in front of you is much more beneficial than dissecting the pathology of addiction through the medical doctor's gaze. For in this relational attunement with individuals suffering with addiction, we can discover the nuances of thought, emotion, and circumstance that have factored into the manifestation of the current addiction. With this deep understanding we can offer therapeutic containment and help the individual find treatment that is best for where they are currently and what they need in this particular moment in their lives.

Critics may say this approach is too philosophical, optimistic, or even impossible to conduct in the real world where habitual drug use, intentional and unintentional overdoses, and life-threatening dangers run rampant. I would argue that any facility, organization, or institution that has ever helped families or clients suffering with addiction has had at least one therapist or practitioner that has embodied the anti-methodology I am proposing. These are the people whose caregiving hearts reign above all else. At the end of the day, they understand that helping those struggling with addiction isn't about a strategic process, a step-by-step system or a workbook method, rather it is about caring, safety, and unconditional positive regard for the human being sitting in front of you. Helping this person see their beauty, strength, resiliency, and empowerment is the key. Letting them know they have not been forgotten and that there is hope no matter what for a life and a future for them filled with joy and peace.

Transmuting Your Pain Into Alchemical Gold

So what should we do with addiction? This is a profound and far more interesting question than "what is addiction?", a question which should have never been asked in the first place. When working with addiction, we must seek to provide it movement. Stagnation, stillness, rigidity, habituation, these are the repetitive death spirals that send people into black holes of despair and darkness. The relentless and obsessive repetition that you can't stop, this is addiction at its worst. We must offer individuals ways out, crevices, cracks, openings, and springboards to freedom. Any expressive form of creativity can offer an opening or a canal of flowing movement. Art, dance, pottery, poetry, spoken word, music, writing, video creation . . . all offer a canal for thoughts, feelings, and emotions to move and flow. These are the arenas that can offer respite and relief from the habitual death spiral, but they require effort, energy, and commitment.

Many practitioners working with addiction will recommend in a very lackluster way that their clients journal, meditate, do yoga, breathwork, etc. However, the essence of what is lost in these clinical recommendations is the creative transmutation which must occur for the individual. What is crucial is that the individual take their pain, anguish, sadness, and despair and channel it into a deeply unique and creative outlet, which only this person can decide for themselves. Each person is different, and this process will require a true idiosyncratic approach for the individual, a trial and error of sorts, with the person undertaking a creative outlet to try and channel the stagnation energy residing in their heart and mind.

If you are going to journal, it must be you creating . . . not copying a format. If you are going to dance, it must be with all your being; if you are going to make music, it must come from your soul; if you are going to write, it must bleed from your fingers. The creative expression must be cathartic and true to who you are, not going through the motions, a true expression of self to channel the energetic stagnation of addiction. In this way, we are able to take the calcified stuckness of habitual addiction and move it to a deterritorialized line of flight.

Understanding Your Complexity

When we begin to see ourselves as a rich array of transcontextual webbings, we are actively beginning to expand the perceptual lenses that create our reality. Many clients struggling with addiction are taught they are broken, damaged, and diseased, and while this may speak to the addictive molar darkness they hold, it in no way represents the entirety of who they are as a human being. All of us are ever-moving, ever-growing, ever-flowing energies of matter and light. Systems interacting, influencing, and warm dataing (Bateson, 2014). If we think we are only one thing, the power of this belief system can truly make us blind to other factions at work in creating our existence. Yes it is true that we are biological beings with an individual psychology, collective socio-cultural society, developmentally growing in the material and spiritual realms, however we are so much more than this. We are cellular energetic beings in a holographic light matrix (Carson, 2019), and when we begin to accept the vastness of our being, we see the patterns, relationships, and shapes that curate our lives.

When I sit with clients, most of my work is helping them recognize the beauty, intricacy, and uniqueness that is themselves. Oftentimes, spending countless sessions with clients to help them unravel the complex false narratives of self-hatred they have created over the years to see their potentiality. Many clients struggling with addiction share they feel out of control and lost in a sea of nihilistic apathy. Anytime they begin to think about "changing," it becomes pointless as they have tried before only to fail and repeat the same patterns of self-destruction and self-abuse/neglect.

Overtime, many clients have created the belief system that they are unable to shift and grow and will forever be doomed to a life of pain and sorrow. However, when we begin to explore in depth the qualities of their being that have kept them alive, functioning and existing, a different story is revealed, a story of persistence, determination, sacrifice, and commitment. These qualities are all beautiful tools that when utilized for self-growth and development can offer a new horizon of truth, clarity, and being. But any forward growth must start with a belief that one is not broken. Whatever hell, pain, anger, loss, sadness, and suffering you have endured it is never too late to take these emotional pools and carve a new canal for them to flow from to allow new healing life water to enter your heart.

Many clients struggling with addiction have lost connection to their first original addiction, maybe it was art, music, sports, dance, science, etc. When they were little, like us all, they were filled with childlike wonder and were artists on this earth, explorers of beauty and experience. However, somewhere along the growth journey many variables came into play which created tension and energetic stagnation. Initially, these individuals found relief, respite, and freedom in a new addiction, that is, drugs, alcohol, sex, video games, shopping, etc. All these methods of consumption tend to leave one empty, vapid, and yearning. But the addictions of creation can satiate parts of the self/soul like no other. So in our work with addiction, we must target the relentless and habitual consumption and turn this energetic engagement into one of expression, creation, and birthing. Consumption will only create molar rigid addiction, rather you must curate and create a way out, a light, an opening, a pathway, a line of flight. But this pathway is one that must be traversed by yourself. Others can show you the path they took, they can share how they built the trail, but each person must create their own trail to addiction recovery. With that being said, the core tenants can remain generalizable both for those struggling with addiction and those working with them:

- Addiction is a multiplistic rhizome, track its movement as it flows rather than treating it as a stagnate entity.

- Addiction lies within each of us, learn to dance with yours and you can help others dance with theirs.
- Addiction will fold in on molar rigidity if methods of consumption increase.
- Addiction can burst into molecular potentiality and lines of flight if true creative and cathartic expression is engaged.
- There is not one methodology to work with addiction, and each person should be understood for how their addiction is manifesting uniquely to them.
- Context is everything, therefore each person experiencing addiction should have a true transcontextual understanding of self or be working with a practitioner/healer or person who can help in guiding this.
- Addiction never goes away, you merely learn how it moves and begin to turn the stagnation into movement.
- Our world comprises addiction both socially and ontologically, we must not fear it, rather we must begin to see its beauty and help others recognize that the components of self they once feared can become their biggest allies.

Do not fear because tomorrow is a new day, and we are pure potentiality waiting to express and explore. If we can see the potential in ourselves, we will always see and invite it in others. Addiction is the tool for which we can burn down our homes and dig our own graves as we destruct and abuse ourselves and others, or the tool for which we can build the most beautiful homes and rebirth ourselves and others by stepping into our unlimited potentiality. Let us seek to continue to build beautiful homes for ourselves and others.

REFERENCES

Alexander, B. K. (2008). *The globalization of addiction: A study in poverty of the spirit*. Oxford University Press.

Alexander, B. K., Beyerstein, B. L., Hadaway, P. F., & Coambs, R. B. (1981). Effect of early and later colony housing on oral ingestion of morphine in rats. *Pharmacology, Biochemistry, and Behavior*, *15*(4), 571–576. https://doi.org/10.1016/0091-3057(81)90211-2

Alexander, F. (1948). *Fundamentals of psychoanalysis*. W. W. Norton.

Alexander, M. (2010). *The new Jim Crow: Mass incarceration in the age of colorblindness*. The New Press.

Allison, H. E. (1987). *Benedict de Spinoza: An introduction* (2nd ed.). Yale University Press.

Arnett, J. J. (1998). Learning to stand alone: The contemporary American transition to adulthood in cultural and historical context. *Human Development*, *41*(5–6), 295–315. https://doi.org/10.1159/000022591

Arnett, J. J. (2000). Emerging adulthood: A theory of development from the late teens through the twenties. *American Psychologist*, *55*(5), 469–480. https://doi.org/10.1037/0003-066X.55.5.469

Arnett, J. J. (2004). *Emerging adulthood: The winding road from the late teens through the twenties*. Oxford University Press.

Asch, S. E. (1952). Group forces in the modification and distortion of judgments. In S. E. Asch (Ed.), *Social psychology* (pp. 450–501). Prentice-Hall. https://doi.org/10.1037/10025-016

Bateson, G. (1972). *Steps to an ecology of mind: Collected essays in anthropology, psychology, evolution, and epistemology*. Chandler Publishing.

Bateson, G. (1975). *Learning to think in a new way* [Keynote address]. Second Lindisfarne Association Conference. www.organism.earth/library/document/learning-to-think-in-a-new-way

Bateson, G. (1979). *Mind and nature: A Necessary unity*. Bantam Books.

Bateson, G. (1991). *Sacred unity: Further steps to an ecology of mind*. Cornelia & Michael Bessie Books.

Bateson, N. (Director). (2010). *An ecology of mind* [Film]. Impact Media Group.

Bateson, N. (2016). *Small arcs of larger circles: Framing through other patterns*. Triarchy Press Limited.

Baumohl, J. (1990). Inebriate institutions in North America, 1840–1920. *British Journal of Addiction*, *85*(9), 1187–1204. https://doi.org/10.1111/j.1360-0443.1990.tb03444.x

Bennett, J. (1984). *A study of Spinoza's ethics*. Hackett Publishing Company.

Berkowitz, L. (1974). Some determinants of impulsive aggression: Role of mediated associations with reinforcements for aggression. *Psychological Review*, *81*(2), 165–176. https://doi.org/10.1037/h0036094

Blake, W. (2008). *The complete poetry and prose of William Blake* (D. Erdman, Ed.). University of California Press.

Blume, A. W., Schmaling, K. B., & Marlatt, G. A. (2000). Revisiting the self-medication hypothesis from a behavioral perspective. *Cognitive and Behavioral Practice*, *7*(4), 379–384. https://doi.org/10.1016/S1077-7229(00)80048-6

Braidotti, R. (2011). *Nomadic subjects: Embodiment and sexual difference in contemporary feminist theory* (2nd ed.). Columbia University Press.

Branson, R. (2012, December 7). War on drugs a trillion-dollar failure. *CNN*. www.cnn.com/2012/12/06/opinion/branson-end-war-on-drugs

Brill, N. Q., Crumpton, E., & Grayson, H. M. (1971). Personality factors in marijuana use. *Archives of General Psychiatry*, *24*, 163–165.

Cannon, M. E. (2009). *Social justice handbook: Small steps for a better world*. IVP Books.

Cardeña, E., & Winkelman, M. (Eds.). (2011). *Altering consciousness: Multidisciplinary perspectives*. Praeger.

Castellanos-Ryan, N., O'Leary-Barrett, M., & Conrod, P. J. (2013). Substance-use in childhood and adolescence: A brief overview of developmental processes and their clinical implications. *Journal of the Canadian Academy of Child and Adolescent Psychiatry*, *22*(1), 41–46.

Chang, H. (2008). *Autoethnography as method*. Left Coast Press.

Chopra, D. (2015). *Quantum healing: Exploring the frontiers of mind/body medicine*. Bantam Books.

Clinton, D. (2003). Rhizome. In G. Deleuze & F. Guattari (Eds.), *A thousand plateaus: Capitalism and schizophrenia*. Theories of Media.

Collective Soul. (1995). The world I know [Song]. In On *collective soul*. Atlantic.

Coonfield, G. (2008). Mapping addicted subjection: Toward a cartography of the addiction epidemic. *Cultural Studies*, *22*(1), 80–113. https://doi.org/10.1080/09502380701480436

Cornford, F. M. (1955). *The republic of Plato*. Oxford University Press.

Coyne, C. J., & Hall, A. R. (2017, April 12). Four decades and counting: The continued failure of the war on drugs. *CATO Institute*. www.cato.org/policy-analysis/four-decades-counting-continued-failure-war-drugs

The Cranberries. (1996). Salvation [Song]. In *On to the faithful departed*. Island Records.

Crocq, M. A. (2007). Historical and cultural aspects of man's relationship with addictive drugs. *Dialogues in Clinical Neuroscience*, *9*(4), 355–361. https://doi.org/10.31887/DCNS.2007.9.4/macrocq

Crossley, N. (1998). R. D. Laing and the British anti-psychiatry movement: A socio-historical analysis. *Social Science & Medicine*, *47*(7), 877–899.

Curley, E. M. (1969). *Spinoza's metaphysics: An essay in interpretation*. Harvard University Press.

Dahl, R. E. (2004). Adolescent brain development: A period of vulnerabilities and opportunities. Keynote address. *Annals of the New York Academy of Sciences*, *1021*, 1–22. https://doi.org/10.1196/annals.1308.001

Darley, J. M., & Latane, B. (1968). Bystander intervention in emergencies: Diffusion of responsibility. *Journal of Personality and Social Psychology*, *8*(4 Pt. 1), 377–383. https://doi.org/10.1037/h0025589

Deleuze, G. (1968). *Difference and repetition*. Presses Universitaires.
Deleuze, G. (1988). *Spinoza: Practical philosophy* (R. Hurley, Trans.). City Light Books. (Original work published 1970)
Deleuze, G. (1992). *Postscript on the societies of control*. MIT Press. www.jstor.org/stable/778828
Deleuze, G., & Guattari, F. (1972). *Anti-Oedipus: Capitalism and schizophrenia*. Penguin Classics.
Deleuze, G., & Guattari, F. (1987). *A thousand plateaus: Capitalism and schizophrenia* (B. Massumi, Trans.). University of Minnesota Press. (Original work published 1980)
Deleuze, G., & Guattari, F. (1994). *What is philosophy?* (H. Tomlinson & G. Burchill, Trans.) Verso. (Original work published 1991)
Eagly, A. H., & Chaiken, S. (1993). *The psychology of attitudes*. Harcourt Brace Jovanovich College Publishers.
Ellis, C., & Bochner, A. (2000). Autoethnography, personal narrative, reflexivity: Researcher as subject. In N. K. Denzin & Y. S. Lincoln (Eds.), *Handbook of qualitative research* (2nd ed., p. 733–768), SAGE Publications.
Ellis, C., Jones, S. H., & Adams, T. E. (Eds.). (2013). *Handbook of autoethnography*. Routledge.
Erikson, E. H. (1993). *Childhood and society*. Norton. (Original work published 1950)
Feinstein, E. C., Richter, L., & Foster, S. E. (2012). Addressing the critical health problem of adolescent substance use through health care, research, and public policy. *The Journal of Adolescent Health*, *50*(5), 431–436. https://doi.org/10.1016/j.jadohealth.2011.12.033
Festinger, L. (1954). A theory of social comparison processes. *Human Relations*, *7*, 117–140. https://doi.org/10.1177/001872675400700202
Foucault, M. (1979). *Discipline and punish: The birth of the prison* (A. Sheridan, Trans.). Vintage.
Frankl, V. (1946). *A man's search for meaning*. Beacon Press.
Gatens, M. (1995). *Imaginary bodies: Ethics, power and corporeality*. Routledge.
Glover, E. (1932). On the aetiology of drug addiction. *The International Journal of Psycho-Analysis*, *13*, 298–328.
Grof, C. (1993). *The thirst for wholeness: Addiction, attachment, and the spiritual path*. HarperCollins.
Günzel, S. (1998, August 10–15). *Immanence and deterritorialization: The philosophy of Gilles Deleuze and Félix Guattari* [Paper presentation]. Twentieth World Congress of Philosophy, Boston, MA. https://doi.org/10.5840/wcp20-paideia19986144
Gustafson, J. (1976). The mirror transference in the psychoanalytic psychotherapy of alcoholism: A case report. *International Journal of Psychoanalytic Psychotherapy*, *5*, 65–85.
Hall, G. S. (1904). *Adolescence: Its psychology and its relations to physiology, anthropology, sociology, sex, crime, religion and education* (Vol. 2). D. Appleton and Company.
Hammer, R., Dingel, M., Ostergren, J., Partridge, B., McCormick, J., & Koenig, B. A. (2013). Addiction: Current criticism of the brain disease paradigm. *AJOB Neuroscience*, *4*(3), 27–32. https://doi.org/10.1080/21507740.2013.796328
Haney, C., Banks, C., & Zimbardo, P. (1973). Interpersonal dynamics in a simulated prison. *International Journal of Criminology & Penology*, *1*(1), 69–97.
Hari, J. (2015). *Chasing the scream: The first and last days of the war on drugs*. Bloomberg Press.
Hart, C. (2013). *High price: A neuroscientist's journey of self-discovery that challenges everything you know about drugs and society*. HarperCollins.
Hergenhahn, B. R. (2005). *An introduction to the history of psychology* (6th ed.). Wadsworth.

Heyman, G. (2010). *Addiction: A disorder of choice*. Harvard University Press.
Hovland, C., Janis, I., & Kelley, H. (1963). *Communication and persuasion: Psychological studies of opinion change*. Yale University Press.
Huba, G. J., Wingard, J. A., & Bentler, P. M. (1981). A comparison of two latent variable causal models for adolescent drug use. *Journal of Personality and Social Psychology, 40*(1), 180–193. https://doi.org/10.1037//0022-3514.40.1.180
Janis, I. L. (1972). *Victims of groupthink: A psychological study of foreign-policy decisions and fiascoes*. Houghton Mifflin.
Johnson, R. A. (1986). *Inner work: Using dreams and active imagination for personal growth*. HarperCollins.
Jung, C. G. (1961). Dr. Carl Jung's letter To Bill W., Jan 30, 1961. *Silkworth.net*. https://silkworth.net/alcoholics-anonymous/dr-carl-jungs-letter-to-bill-w-jan-30–1961
Jung, C. G. (1969). *On the nature of the psyche* (R. F. C. Hull, Trans.). Princeton University Press.
Kerouac, J. (1957). *On the road*. The Viking Press.
Kim, D.-J. (1987). *Prison writings* (Choi Sung-il & David R. McCann, Trans.). University of California Press.
King County Bar Association. (2005). *Drugs and the drug laws: Historical and cultural contexts*. www.kcba.org/kcba/druglaw/pdf/report_hc.pdf
Krystal, H. (1978). Trauma and affects. *The Psychoanalytic Study of the Child, 33*, 81–116. https://doi.org/10.1080/00797308.1978.11822973
Laing, R. D. (1971). *The politics of the family and other essays*. Tavistock.
Leonard, L. S. (2001). *Witness to the fire: Creativity & the veil of addiction*. Shambala.
Lipton, B. H. (2016). *The biology of belief: Unleashing the power of consciousness, matter and miracles* (10th anniversary ed.). Mountain of Love Productions.
Lorraine, T. (2005). Lines of flight. In A. Parr (Ed.), *The Deleuze dictionary* (pp. 147–148). Edinburgh University Press.
Martel, Y. (2001). *Life of pi*. Harcourt, Inc.
Maslow, A. H. (1965). Humanistic science and transcendent experiences. *Journal of Humanistic Psychology, 5*(2), 219–227. https://doi.org/10.1177/002216786500500211
May, R. (Ed.). (1961). *Existential psychology*. Random House.
McDougall, W. (2003). *An introduction to social psychology*. Dover Publications. (Original work published 1908)
McKenzie, P. J. (2003). A model of information practices in accounts of everyday-life information seeking. *Journal of Documentation, 59*(1), 19–40. https://doi.org/10.1108/00220410310457993
Milgram, S. (1974). *Obedience to authority: An experimental view*. Harper & Row.
Miller, W. R., & Carroll, K. M. (Eds.). (2006). *Rethinking substance abuse: What the science shows, and what we should do about it*. Guilford Press.
Morgan, O. (1999). *Addiction and spirituality: A multidisciplinary approach*. Chalice Press.
Murray, H. A. (1981). American Icarus. In E. S. Shneidman (Ed.), *Endeavors in psychology: Selections from the personology of Henry A. Murray* (pp. 535–556). Harper & Row. (Original work published 1955)
Nadler, S. (2020). *Think least of death: Spinoza on how to live and how to die*. Princeton University Press.
Nathan, P. E., Conrad, M., & Skinstad, A. H. (2016). History of the concept of addiction. *Annual Review of Clinical Psychology, 12*, 29–51. https://doi.org/10.1146/annurev-clinpsy-021815-093546
National Institute on Drug Abuse. (2014). *Principles of adolescent substance use disorder treatment: A research-based guide introduction*. https://nida.nih.gov/publications/principles-adolescent-substance-use-disorder-treatment-research-based-guide/introduction

National Institute on Drug Abuse. (2020, July 13). *Drug misuse and addiction*. https://nida.nih.gov/publications/drugs-brains-behavior-science-addiction/drug-misuse-addiction on 2022

Neale, J., Parkin, S., Hermann, L., Metrebian, N., Roberts, E., Robson, D., & Strang, J. (2022). Substance use and homelessness: A longitudinal interview study conducted during COVID-19 with implications for policy and practice. *International Journal of Drug Policy*, *108*, 1–10. https://doi.org/10.1016/j.drugpo.2022.103818

Nixon, R. (1971, June 17). *Remarks about an intensified program for drug abuse prevention and control*. The American Presidency Project. www.presidency.ucsb.edu/documents/remarks-about-intensified-program-for-drug-abuse-prevention-and-control

Oksanen, A. (2013). Female rock stars and addiction in autobiographies. *Nordic Studies on Alcohol and Drugs*, *30*(1–2), 123–140.

Online Etymology Dictionary. (2022). *Psychology*. www.etymonline.com/word/psychology

Orford, J. (2002). Addiction as excessive appetite. *Addiction*, *96*(1), 15–31. https://doi.org/10.1046/j.1360-0443.2001.961152.x

Oxford English Dictionary. (1884). *Addiction*. Oxford English Dictionary.

Pedersen, W. (1991). Mental health, sensation seeking and drug use patterns: A longitudinal study. *British Journal of Addiction*, *86*(2), 195–204. https://doi.org/10.1111/j.1360-0443.1991.tb01769.x

Piaget, J. (1977). *Epistemology and psychology of functions*. D. Reidel Publishing Company.

Radó, S. (1933). The psychoanalysis of pharmacothymia (drug addiction). *The Psychoanalytic Quarterly*, *2*, 1–23.

Ram Dass, B. (1971). *Be here now*. HarperCollins.

Red Hot Chili Peppers. (1991). Soul to squeeze [Song]. In *On blood sugar sex magik*. Warner Bros. Records.

Red Hot Chili Peppers. (2006). Snow (hey oh) [Song]. In *On stadium arcadium*. Warner Records.

Riley, G. (2011). Pursuit of integrated living: The fair housing act as a sword for mentally disabled adults residing in group homes. *Columbia Journal of Law and Social Problems*, *45*, 177–224. http://jlsp.law.columbia.edu/wp-content/uploads/sites/8/2017/03/45-Riley.pdf

Robins, L. N. (1993). Vietnam veterans' rapid recovery from heroin addiction: A fluke or normal expectation? *Addiction*, *88*(8), 1041–1054. https://doi.org/10.1111/j.1360-0443.1993.tb02123.x

Robins, L. N., Davis, D. H., & Nurco, D. N. (1974). How permanent was Vietnam drug addiction? *American Journal of Public Health*, *64*(12), S38–S43. https://doi.org/10.2105/ajph.64.12_suppl.38

Rogers, C. R. (1959). A theory of therapy, personality, and interpersonal relationships: As developed in the client-centered framework. In S. Koch (Ed.), *Psychology: A study of a science. Formulations of the person and the social context* (vol. 3, pp. 184–256). McGraw-Hill.

Rogers, C. R. (2015). *On becoming a person*. Mariner Books.

Ross, E. A. (1974). *Social psychology*. Arno Press. (Original work published 1908)

Ruiz, D. M. (2010). *The mastery of love: A practical guide to the art of relationship*. Amber-Allen Publishing.

Rush, B. (1784). *An inquiry into the effects of ardent spirits upon the human body and mind*. James Loring.

Rush, B. (1947). The effects of ardent spirits upon man. In D. D. Runes (Ed.), *The selected writings of Benjamin Rush* (pp. 344–341). Philosophical Library. (Original work published 1805)

Sabirsh, J. (2017). *Love all-knowing: An epic spiritual poem*. www.loveallknowing.com

Sartre, J.-P. (2007). *Existentialism is a humanism*. Éditions Gallimard. (Original work published 1945)

Sayin, H. U. (2014). Does the nervous system have an intrinsic archaic language? Entoptic images and phosphenes. *NeuroQuantology*, *12*(3), 427–445.

Scott, J., & Marshall, G. (2009). *Oxford dictionary of sociology* (4th rev. ed.). Oxford University Press.

Sherif, M. (1936). *The psychology of social norms.* Harper & Row.

Shin, S. H., Chung, Y., & Jeon, S. M. (2013). Impulsivity and substance use in young adulthood. *The American Journal on Addictions*, *22*(1), 39–45. https://doi.org/10.1111/j.1521-0391.2013.00324.x

Silkworth, W. D. (1937). *Alcoholism as a manifestation of allergy.* https://silkworth.net/alcoholics-anonymous/alcoholism-as-a-manifestation-of-allergy

Skott-Myhre, H. (2006). Radical youth work: Becoming visible. *Child and Youth Care Forum*, *35*, 219–229. https://doi.org/10.1007/s10566-006-9010-2

Skott-Myhre, H. (2008). *Youth and subculture as creative force: Creating new spaces for radical youth work.* University of Toronto Press.

Skott-Myhre, K. (2016). Youth: A radical space of pilgrimage. In H. Skott-Myhre, V. Pacini-Ketchabaw, & K. Skott-Myhre (Eds.), *Youth work, early education, and psychology: Liminal encounters* (pp. 179–193). Palgrave MacMillan.

Smith, A. R., Chein, J., & Steinberg, L. (2014). Peers increase adolescent risk taking even when the probabilities of negative outcomes are known. *Developmental Psychology*, *50*(5), 1564–1568. https://doi.org/10.1037/a0035696

Spinoza, B. (2009). *Ethics* (R. H. M. Elwes, Trans.). The Floating Press. (Original work published 1677)

Stangor, C., & Walinga, J. (2014). *Introduction to psychology.* BC Campus Open Education. https://opentextbc.ca/introductiontopsychology/

Steinberg, L. (2001). We know some things: Parent—adolescent relationships in retrospect and prospect. *Journal of Research and Adolescence*, *11*(1), 1–19. https://doi.org/10.1111/1532-7795.00001

Tantam, D. (1991). The anti-psychiatry movement. In G. E. Berrios and H. Freeman (Eds.), *150 years of British psychiatry* (pp. 333–347). Gaskell.

Triplett, N. (1898). The dynamogenic factors in pacemaking and competition. *American Journal of Psychology*, *9*(4), 507–533. https://doi.org/10.2307/1412188

Tupes, E. C., & Christal, R. E. (1992). Recurrent personality factors based on trait ratings. *Journal of Personality*, *60*(2), 225–251. https://doi.org/10.1111/j.1467-6494.1992.tb00973.x

Vetulani, J. (2001). Drug addiction. Part I. Psychoactive substances in the past and presence. *Polish Journal of Pharmacology*, *53*(3), 201–214.

Wallis, C., & Park, A. (2004, May 10). What makes teens tick. *Time*, *163*(19), 56–65. https://time.com/620/what-makes-teens-tick

Watts, A. (1951). *The wisdom of insecurity: A message for an age of anxiety.* Pantheon Books.

Watts, A. (1973). *In my own way: An autobiography.* Vintage.

Watts, A. (2017). *In the academy: Essays and lectures.* SUNY Press.

West, R. (2006). *Theory of addiction.* Blackwell Publishing.

White, W. L. (2000). The role of recovering physicians in 19th century addiction medicine: An organizational case study. *Journal of Addictive Diseases*, *19*(2), 1–10. https://doi.org/10.1300/J069v19n02_01

White, W. L. (2004). History of drug problems and drug policies in America. In R. Coombs (Ed.), *Addiction counseling review: Preparing for comprehensive certification exams* (pp. 81–104). Lahaska Press.

White, W. L. (2010). *Relapse is NOT a part of recovery: A brief commentary.* www.chestnut.org/Resources/33827e78-6bbe-4259-9751-1f87dc612205/2010-Relapse-is-NOT-Part-of-Recovery.pdf

White, W. L. (2014). *Slaying the dragon: The history of addiction treatment and recovery in America* (2nd ed.). Chestnut Health Systems/Lighthouse Institute.

Wilber, K. (2000). Waves, streams, states, and self. Further considerations for an integral theory of consciousness. *Journal of Consciousness Studies*, *7*(11–12), 145–176.

Wolff, C. (2010). *Psychologia empirica methodo scientifica pertractata*. Kessinger Publishing. (Original work published 1732)

Wurmser, L. (1974). Psychoanalytic considerations of the etiology of compulsive drug use. *Journal of the American Psychoanalytic Association*, *22*(4), 820–843. https://doi.org/10.1177/000306517402200407

Yalisove, D. L. (Ed.). (1997). *Essential papers on addiction*. New York University Press.

Yalom, I. D. (1980). *Existential psychotherapy*. Basic Books.

Yates, R., & Malloch, M. S. (2010). The road less travelled? A short history of addiction recovery. In R. Yates & M. S. Malloch (Eds.), *Tackling addiction: Pathways to recovery* (pp. 15–31). Jessica Kingsley Publishers.

Zoja, L. (2000). *Drugs, addiction and initiation: The modern search for ritual* (M. E. Romano & R. Mercurio, Trans.). Daimon.

Zuckerman, M., Murtaugh, T., & Siegel, J. (1974). Sensation seeking and cortical augmenting-reducing. *Psychophysiology*, *11*(5), 535–542. https://doi.org/10.1111/j.1469-8986.1974.tb01109.x

INDEX

Note: Page numbers in *italic* indicate a figure on the corresponding page.

For Product Safety Concerns and Information please contact our EU
representative GPSR@taylorandfrancis.com
Taylor & Francis Verlag GmbH, Kaufingerstraße 24, 80331 München, Germany

www.ingramcontent.com/pod-product-compliance
Ingram Content Group UK Ltd.
Pitfield, Milton Keynes, MK11 3LW, UK
UKHW020000200926
475702UK00015B/2395
* 9 7 8 1 0 3 2 7 3 8 0 8 6 *